May

(oct 1, 71.)

THE DOG LOVER'S LIBRARY

Edited by *CLIFFORD L. B. HUBBARD*

THE BLOODHOUND HANDBOOK

A

THE DOG LOVER'S LIBRARY

Edited by

CLIFFORD L. B. HUBBARD

A series of breed handbooks each written by an authority of general or specialist repute, and copiously illustrated with engravings, prints and photographs of important early and modern dogs. Each book is an up-to-date monograph on a particular breed or variety. Crown octavo, illustrated, 7s. 6d. net.

Other titles include

THE DACHSHUND HANDBOOK
THE STAFFORDSHIRE BULL TERRIER HANDBOOK
THE BOXER HANDBOOK
THE AFGHAN HOUND HANDBOOK
THE COCKER SPANIEL HANDBOOK
THE PEKINGESE HANDBOOK
THE SCOTTISH TERRIER HANDBOOK
THE PEMBROKESHIRE CORGI HANDBOOK
THE CARDIGANSHIRE CORGI HANDBOOK
THE WHIPPET HANDBOOK
THE DALMATIAN HANDBOOK
THE BORZOI HANDBOOK
THE GOLDEN RETRIEVER HANDBOOK
THE BULL TERRIER HANDBOOK
THE BULLMASTIFF HANDBOOK
THE ENGLISH SETTER HANDBOOK
THE BULLDOG HANDBOOK
THE CAIRN TERRIER HANDBOOK
THE PUG HANDBOOK
THE WIRE-HAIRED FOX TERRIER HANDBOOK
THE PAPILLON HANDBOOK
THE DANDIE DINMONT TERRIER HANDBOOK
THE BEAGLE HANDBOOK
THE WELSH TERRIER HANDBOOK
THE YORKSHIRE TERRIER HANDBOOK
THE ENGLISH SPRINGER SPANIEL HANDBOOK
THE BASSET HOUND HANDBOOK
THE SHETLAND SHEEPDOG HANDBOOK

Bronze by J. B. Gélibert of " Druid ", the first Champion Bloodhound.
No. 17 in the *Stud Book* he was born in 1857 and was bought by
Napoleon III for his son Eugéne Louis Jean Joseph.

THE
BLOODHOUND
HANDBOOK

GIVING THE HISTORY, POINTS AND BREEDING OF THE
SHOW DOG, SECTIONS ON WORKING AND TRIALS,
AND A NOTE ON DISTENTION BY
R. S. TOWNSON, M.R.C.V.S.

BY

DOUGLAS H. APPLETON

NICHOLSON & WATSON

LONDON

First published in 1960

Printed in GREAT BRITAIN
by
LOVE & MALCOMSON, LTD.
London and Redhill

PREFACE

THE Bloodhound has a noble history, and above his head hovers a halo of romance. There have also been occasions when the prospect of extinction has hovered above him . . . and it is then that he has found his truest friends.

No breed can vigorously thrive on the strength of past greatness, nor can it always rely on finding financially able and generous backers as it has in the past. The breed cannot thrive solely by its presence at dog shows and occasional Field Trials. Those who love these hounds must breed for good temperament, for active brains, and for the ability to fit into the home life of to-day. In order to do so some exaggerations of type may have to be swept away, but this price would prove well worth while.

My thanks are due to many friends who have helped with the notes of their hounds, and especially to the Kennel Club and the American Kennel Club for documentary assistance, Mrs. Yvonne Oldman for the loan of some most interesting scrapbooks, and to Mr. Clifford Hubbard for his usual help with historical material and illustrations. I hope this volume will provoke thought and discussion which is wholly constructive, and therefore helpful to the breed.

DOUGLAS H. APPLETON.

OULTON, *June*, 1959.

v

[Mr. Appleton is the author of *The Beagle Handbook* and *The Basset Hound Handbook* published in this series—*Editor*.]

CONTENTS

CHAPTER   PAGE

I. ORIGIN AND HISTORY 1
The St. Hubert Hound—Early Manhunts—
Early Breeders

II. RECENT HISTORY AND GOVERNMENT . . . 13
Post-war Importations—Bloodhounds Around
the World—Popularising the Breed—Records—
Governing Bodies—Leading Kennels

III. THE STANDARD 29
American Standard—Analysis—Movement—
Breed Points—Measurements—Judges

IV. THE PET BLOODHOUND 45
House Training—Teaching His Name—Lead
Training—'No' and 'Sit'

V. BREEDING AND FEEDING 56
Choosing a Sire—Breeding Contracts—Mating
—Choosing the Dam—Whelping—The Young
Puppy—Feeding

VI. BREED PROBLEMS AND CARE 77
Distention—Inverted Eyelids—Temperament—
External Care

VII. TRAINING TRIALS 89
Training to Hunt—Working Trials—K.C. Trial
Rules—Hunting Aids—The Horn—The Har-
ness—The Huntsman

VIII. GLOSSARY OF BLOODHOUND TERMS . . . 105

IX. HOUND NAMES 118

INDEX 126

ILLUSTRATIONS

Frontispiece: Bronze by J. B. Gélibert of " Druid ", the
first Champion Bloodhound. No. 17 in the *Stud
Book* he was born in 1857 and was bought by
Napoleon III for his son Eugéne Louis Jean Joseph.

Facing page

PLATE I 18
Bloodhound on the trail, by Reinagle, 1820: Bloodhounds by Sydenham Teak Edwards, 1800: 'Bloodhounds on the Trail ', by G. B. Goddard, 1878.

PLATE II 19
Sir Edwin Landseer's ' Sleeping Bloodhound ' (Jacob
Bell's " Countess "), 1835: Landseer's ' Shoeing the
Bay Mare ' (with " Laura "), 1844: Landseer's
' Dignity and Impudence ' (with " Grafton "), 1839.

PLATE III 34
Briton Rivière's ' Last of the Garrison ', 1875:
Rivière's ' In Manus Tua Domine ', 1879.

PLATE IV 35
Six famous early Hounds: Rev. G. Straton's "Luath
XI "; G. R. Krehl's Ch. " Cromwell "; H. G. H.
Sandeman's Ch. " Blazer "; E. Brough's " Bur-
gundy"; E. Brough's Ch. "Barbarossa"; A. Croxton
Smith's " Panther ".

Facing page

PLATE V 50
    Capt. and Mrs. C. H. Chapman with a ' Radnage'
    quartet, *c.* 1903: R. H. Moore's drawing of Ch.
    " Margrave ", *c.* 1905: Brough's Chs. " Barnaby "
    and " Burgho ", by L. Boellaars, 1894.

PLATE VI 51
    Ch. " Dark of Brighton ", winner of 31 C.Cs., bred
    by the late Henry Hylden: " Chatley Brilliant ",
    mounted at the British Museum of Natural History:
    Black-and-tan American Coonhounds.

PLATE VII 66
    The celebrated " Nick Carter ", a Bloodhound re-
    sponsible for over 600 American arrests and con-
    victions: Lady Waverley's " Dusk of Westsummer-
    land " with Chs. " Coral " and " Emily ": Mr. and
    Mrs. Oliphants' Ch. " Chatley Blazer ", by Emms,
    1905.

PLATE VIII 67
    Mr. H. S. Lloyd with a brace of 4½ months' pup-
    pies: English Bloodhounds, an American Blood-
    hound, and Bloodhound—Otterhound crosses, at the
    ' of Ware ' training kennels: The Dumfriesshire Fox-
    hounds, a pack of black-and-tan hounds.

PLATE IX 74
    Mr. and Mrs. R. Furness' W.T. Ch. " Raycroft
    Sailer " after the painting by Evelyn Barnsley: Mrs.
    M. Sadleir's Ch. " Barset of Barchester "; Mrs. Y.
    Oldman with Ch. " Barsheen Jewel ".

Facing page

PLATES X and XI . . . . 74 & 75
    Head studies of "Cromwell" (after a painting by
    Maud Earl) and the author's Ch. " Appeline Hector
    of Westsummersland "; Ch. " Dominator of Brigh-
    ton ", owned by Mr. Hylden: Ch. " Scarcity of
    Kelperland ", owned by Mr. Townson: Mr. Douglas
    Henderson, of Brisbane, with Chs. " Pluto " and
    " Wuthering Dulciana of Dobrudden ".

PLATE XII   75
    The author's Int. Ch. " Spotter of Littlebrook ",
    winner 41 times out of 42 in the U.S.A. and never
    beaten by a dog in Britain: Mr. and Mrs. A. Lang-
    dale's D. Ch. " Easebourne Tarquin ", the only post-
    war Dual Champion: Mrs. Oldfield and Mr. Nichols'
    Ch. " Dasher of Brighton ", the only Bloodhound to
    go BiS at a post-war championship show.

PLATE XIII   98
    One of Mrs. G. A. Woodall's " Ben Jairg " exports
    to the U.S.A.: Am. Ch. " Appeline Hemlock "
    owned by Mr. Kent McClelland of the American
    Bloodhound Club: Mr. J. Gilissen's Hubertus Pack,
    which hunts fox in Holland.

PLATE XIV   99
    Dr. Ballard's Can. Ch. " Appeline Barsheen Hunts-
    man " smells his last English Spring: Mr. G. L.
    Gilkey of Wisconsin with one of his working Blood-
    hounds: Mrs. N. Lindsey and Ch. " The Ring's
    Imp " winning Hound group under Dr. A. A.
    Mitten, Duso K.C., June, 1958.

Facing page

PLATE XV 114
Ch. " Easebourne Argos " owned by Det. Sgt. Erik
E. Pettersson of Oedeshoeg, Sweden—Mr. Pettersson
has the largest kennel and trains hounds for the
Swedish police: Mr. Poul Lassen with Ch. " Buxhall
Annette ", Mr. Pettersson with " Astor's Donna
Urvana ", and Mr. Herluf Anderson with " Hazel
of Brighton ", at the Danish K.C. show, Copen-
hagen, November, 1958.

PLATE XVI 115
Puppies out of Ch. " Bonnie ", owned by Mr. and
Mrs. Boland of New York: British television
comedian Benny Hill and Ch. " Hector " on the
trail—with apologies to Sexton Blake and " Pedro "
—in the Michael Balcon-Ealing Studios production
' Who Done It? '.

CHAPTER I

ORIGIN AND EARLY HISTORY

BRITISH-BRED Bloodhounds are to-day the finest in the world, and overseas stock, wherever shown or working, traces its descent from animals exported from Britain. In fact with exports of all breeds so much in the news it can almost be said that the first canine sales in the export drive were made when Ancient Britons frequently sold hounds with Bloodhound characteristics to Gaul and elsewhere on the European mainland.

To go right back to the grand originals, the family tree of the Bloodhound can be traced as follows. Starting, as all the canines, with *Tormarctos*, a small animal which lived fifteen or more million years ago, we progress to one of the four earliest dog types—the *Canis familiaris leineri* which had developed by 6000 B.C. From here through the Egyptian Greyhound and Afghan Hound, to the Sleuth Hound, and thence via the St. Hubert and the Talbot Hounds we progressed to the Bloodhound in its present form. Of the Bloodhound's forbears all but the Afghan are extinct, and from the Bloodhound and the Russian Tracker the Golden Retriever was evolved.

Our early forbears were not agriculturalists to any marked degree and depended for their food upon their success as hunters. The hunting was primitive and great reliance had to be placed on the scenting and fighting powers of the dogs of the chase.

1

The best game-finding hounds were keenly sought after by early chieftains and medieval princes, and while no dog shows as we know them existed at that time to encourage or define type, the more noble looking hounds were the most highly valued.

Hounds similar in character as we know them to-day have been referred to as Brache, Limier, Saint Hubert Sleuth (Slot or Slough), or Talbot Hounds, by early historians.

The St. Hubert Hound

Overall an aura of romance covers the hounds, and that of St. Hubert is the most romantic. The legend tells that a nobleman, Francois Hubert, hunting with his hounds on a Good Friday, saw a vision of a stag with a glittering cross growing between its antlers. This vision induced him to give up his dissipated life, to become a monk, and, in 687, to found an abbey. He became the Bishop of Liège and was later canonised the patron saint of sportsmen. In the Ardennes, at St. Hubert's Abbey, the breed was for many centuries kept in his memory, and even up to the time of the French Revolution the abbots sent annual drafts to the French kings. The legend has been immortalised by a number of paintings by the great Masters, the best known being that by Pisanello, which can be seen at the National Gallery and is reproduced in *The Book of the Dog*.

In France and Belgium the hounds are still known as Chiens de Saint-Hubert, and in some parts of these countries and of Ireland, the traditional ceremony of blessing the hounds still takes place at the start of each hunting season. French writers say these hounds were either black or white, the latter being the least popular as they only hunted the stag.

The trend of the movement later swung in a complete circle, and French sovereigns and sportsmen sent hounds to Queen Elizabeth, James I and Henry IV. The white hounds seem to have been still known in England after they were extinct in France. There are English oil paintings depicting black-and-tan, red and light grey hounds. Some writers have attributed this latter colour to artistic licence but this is wrong as it probably came from the white St. Huberts [or the Grey hounds of St. Louis, which flourished from about 1250 to 1500?—*Editor*].

Black-and-tan is recorded as being the colour of the pack of Cardinal de Guise and, as far as I have been able to ascertain, the liver is first recorded in the middle of the sixteenth century.

EARLY MANHUNTS

The following is an interesting historical record of British Bloodhounds being used for hunting man:

In the reign of James I all Galloway, and as time went on, all Scotland was thrilled, horrified, and puzzled by the mysterious disappearances of travellers from a stretch of country near the coast.

The travellers set forth, but never arrived, and the searchers found no traces. Innkeepers and others were suspected, and some of these unfortunate wretches were roughly tried and executed.

But the disappearances continued—continued in fact, for the space of more than a generation. Then on a summers evening, a farmer and his wife, who

B

was riding pillion, were returning from a fair when they were ambushed by a band of horrible looking beings, of all ages. The farmer sought to charge through them, but some of them seized and tore his wife from the horse, and before his eyes slit her throat—and drank of the blood. After which they proceeded to cut her up. Though fighting like a fury, the farmer must soon have suffered a like fate, had not a party of people also returned from the fete, appeared in sight. Thereupon the horrible band fled, taking the body with them. The country-side was roused, the King himself was summoned yet for a time it seemed that the murderers had dis-appeared as completely as their victim.

Bloodhounds were obtained, and the hunt was extended to the shore under the cliffs with their many caves. The hunters would have passed one cave, which as was obvious, was flooded at high water, but now the tide was low. And suddenly the hounds became excited, the hunters proceeded into and up the cave, which was of such depth that they were at last thinking of turning back, when in a great chamber, dimly lit by smoky wicks, they came upon Sawney Bean, his woman and their progeny, of twenty-five years. The habitation was a store-house of human apparel, weapons, money and so forth, of horse accoutrements, and all manner of merchandise.

But, more than that—it was a larder; on the rocky walls were plentyous supplies of food, in the shape of human limbs, smoked or pickled in brine. For you see Mr. Bean and his family were canni-bals. . . . For the credit of Galloway it must be said that Mr. Bean was not a native, he had come from

—no, I had better suppress his original address. To conclude, the dreadful crew, forty-eight in all, counting grandchildren, were taken to Edinburgh, then to Leith, where the males, their hands and feet amputated, were bled to death and the females burned; they died cursing and swearing.

During the next two hundred years hounds of the Bloodhound type are mentioned in quite a number of French and English writings, but never by this name.

In the early 1600's the border counties of Cumberland, Northumberland and Westmorland were much worried by Scottish politics. In September 1616 the following warrant was issued to the garrison at Carlisle, giving orders as to the keeping of ' Slough dogs '.

Whereas upon due consideration of the increase of stealths, daily growing both in deed and report among you on the borders, we formally concluded and agreed, that for reformations therefor, to the contents of His Majesty's directions to us in that behalf prescribed; and for that, according to our agreement, Sir William Hutton, at his last being in the country, did appoint how the watches should be kept, when and where they should begin, and how they might best and most fitly continue. And for the bettering of His Majesty's service, and preventing further danger that might ensue by the outlaws in resorting to the houses of Thomas Routledge, alias Balihead, being nearest and next adjoining to the Marshes (he himself having also joined them—as is reported), order and direction were likewise given, that some of the garrison should keep and reside in his the said Thomas Routledge's house; and there to remain until further directions be given them, unless he the said Thomas Routledge shall come in and enter himself answerable to His Majesty's law, as is most convenient. . . . and that you see that Slough dogs be provided according to our former directions, as this note to this warrant annexed particularly sets down.

Without quoting the whole of the warrant, it may be stated that six other ' Slough dogs ' were ordered to be provided and kept at the expense of the following parishes, one dog in each:

Newcastle, Stapleton, Irdington; Lanercost and Walton; Kirklington, Scaleby, Houghton and Rickarby; and Westlington; Roucliff, Etterby, Staunton, Stanix and Cargo, to be kept at Roucliff.

Moving on again through history, it becomes apparent that hounds of the Bloodhound type must have been very plentiful, for in 1795 no less than 200 were sent to Jamaica to assist in quelling a resistance of the Maroons. The arrival of the hounds so terrorized the poor devils that they immediately surrendered.

Just over a century ago, by which time a type similar to that which we know of to-day was beginning to be established, *The Field* published the following:

Tom Finkle, an old superintendent of police, was stationed at Bedale, in Yorkshire, before the rural force was established. He was the owner of a Bloodhound named Voltigeur. Old Tom was fond of company, and at that time sat for many a night in the public-houses along with the farmers and tradesmen. When he was wanted for anything particular at the police station, Mrs. Finkle would let

Voltigeur loose with, ' Go and fetch master ', and, no matter where ' master ' was, either in Bedale or the neighbourhood, the hound was sure to find him; and the moment Finkle saw Voltigeur, the old superintendent knew he was required at the station.

In the winter of 1854, or early in 1855, certain burglars broke into a house at Askern, and stole a quantity of silver plate and linen. The burglars, heard by the inmates of the house, had to decamp rather hurriedly, and a messenger was immediately sent to the police station to report the outrage. Old Tom was, as usual, with his companions at the Royal Oak, whilst his wife was in bed. The latter immediately got up and turned Voltigeur loose, with the order, ' Go and fetch master '. The hound was not long in doing his duty, and Tom, jumping off his seat, said to his friends, ' I am wanted at home ', and hurried there as quickly as possible. His wife reported the circumstances of the robbery to her husband, who at once called his constable and saddled his horse.

The two then started off to the scene of the robbery, and after visiting the house and learning all particulars, they went outside. When in the grounds, Finkle said to Voltigeur, ' Where are they? ', ' Seek 'em ', and Voltigeur, putting his nose to the ground, took up the scent and went away at a nice pace, every now and then giving tongue. The night being calm, Voltigeur's voice was heard by many. The hound made out the line of the robbers on to the High-street leading from Boroughbridge to Catterick, and after going about three miles on the High-street he stopped suddenly at a small watercourse that ran under the road. The superintendent dismounted and looked under the bridge, where he found a bundle containing a quantity of linen and silver plate, part of the proceeds of the robbery. He waited there for a time until his man came up, then, remounting, ordered his hound on again. Voltigeur put his nose to the ground, and went back along the same road he had come for about a mile. Then through a gate he made his way to an outbarn and buildings.

Here the Bloodhound became more excited, and was baying and giving tongue freely as his owner and his man got up. The superintendent went to the one door, and the constable to the other. The former demanded admittance, but all was still as death, and the doors fast. Tom looked about the buildings and found a crowbar, and was then soon into the barn, where he discovered two men concealed in the straw. They appealed for mercy, and prayed to him to keep the dog off, and they would yield themselves up quietly. The prisoners were then secured and searched, and upon them was found the remainder of the stolen property. They were taken to Bedale, locked up for the night, next day brought before the magistrates and committed to the assizes, where they were sentenced to five years' penal servitude each, there being previous convictions against them. Voltigeur was of the Duke of Leeds' strain of Bloodhounds, some of which were at that time kept at Hornby Castle.

From this time onwards hounds were quite widely used to assist in catching poachers.

EARLY BREEDERS

In 1878 ' Stonehenge ' (J. H. Walsh), one of the first dog show judges and an editor of *The Field*, wrote in his third edition of *The Dogs of the British Islands*:

Until within the last twenty years, or thereabouts, the bloodhound has been almost entirely confined to the kennels of the English nobility; but at about that distance of time Mr. Jennings, of Pickering, in Yorkshire, obtained a draft or two from Lord Faversham and Baron Rothschild, and in a few years, by his skill and care, produced his Druid and Welcome, a magnificent couple of hounds, which he afterwards sold, at what was then considered a high price, to Prince Napoleon for breeding purposes. In the course of time, and probably from the fame acquired by these dogs at the various shows, his example was followed by his north-country neighbours, Major Cowen and Mr. J. W. Pease, who monopolised the prizes of the show bench with successive Druids, descended from Mr. Jennings' dog of that name, and aided by Draco, Dingle, Dauntless, &c., all of the same strain. . . . In 1869, however, another candidate for fame appeared in Mr. Holford's Regent, a magnificent dog, both in shape and colour, but still of the same strains, and, until the appearance of Mr. Reynold Ray's Roswell in 1870, no fresh blood was introduced among the first-prize winners at our chief shows. . . . This dog, who died last year, maintained his position for the same period almost without dispute, and even in his old age it took a good dog to beat him.

It was actually in 1860 that Bloodhounds were first admitted at a dog show. This was at Birmingham, the show which now proudly celebrates its centenary. On this occasion the principal winners were Mr. Jenning's " Druid " and Lord Bigot's bitch " Rapid ".

Competitive Working Trials started much later. The Association of Bloodhound Breeders being the first in 1898 when Sir Charles Legard judged and the Oliphant's " Chatley Regent " was the main winner.

The Bloodhound Club did not hold its first Trials until 1903, when Mr. Jake Scarlett, Master of the Tedworth, and Mr. W. H. Dunn, Master of the Craven judged. Reports indicate that conditions were difficult and really testing, but in spite of this a dozen hounds gained certificates of merit.

In the last 100 years the history of the breed has been made by men or women who have put the good of the hound before any personal gain and contemporary breeders have been left a precious heritage. As we go through the early part of the century the names of the great Edward Brough, T. A. Jennings, Field and Cousens, Lord Bagot, J. C. Tinker, Mrs. S. A. Humphries and Miss S. T. Heydon come readily to mind, so great was their influence. The Brough Cup is still awarded at Field Trials, his wonderful scrap books are in the keeping of the Kennel Club, and undoubtedly his was the greatest single contribution to Bloodhound progress.*

---

* Edward Brough was indeed the king of Bloodhound breeders, reigning for over half a century. To-day, when there are over 150,000 dogs entered in the *Kennel Club Stud Book* it is with pride we consult volume 1 and find that Class 1 is devoted to Bloodhounds, where from Nos. 1-71 appear many of the most famous names in the breed. And as the Bloodhound was first in both the Calendar and the Register so too was Edward Brough in the first and almost

As we come to the start of the twentieth century we find Brough still carrying on, supported by C. J. B. Moneypenny, Mrs. S. H. Mangin—Mrs. Mangin and Mrs. C. Ashton Cross are more famous to-day for the Peke (see *The Pekingese Handbook* in this series), vastly different in size but none the less noble in spirit— and throughout this period the Oliphants and the Hyldens too who have bred Bloodhounds for four generations.

Latterly we have had Viscount and Viscountess Waverley (Sir John Anderson), the late Mrs. N. E. Elms, Mrs. M. Sadlier, Mrs. Harris St. John, all doing sterling work. Mrs. Elms will, of course, be always remembered for her celebrated Ch. " Leo of Reynolton ", one of the greatest of the hounds bred in the 1920's. In this packed period of the breed history there must be some names I have missed but the breeders of to-day are grateful for the efforts of all.

The contemporary kennels are in their turn maintaining the breed but their achievements and reputations will be judged and their place in breed history fixed not by the number of C.Cs. won or by the array of cups in their trophy rooms, but by the good they have done the breed as a whole.

---

every volume of this gigantic record of the nineteenth and twentieth century. Brough was also a prolific writer on his breed.

Other giants in the Bloodhound world, working alongside with Brough with breeding plan, trail leash and with pen, included Arthur Croxton Smith, onetime secretary of the Kennel Club and author of many books on dogs; Major Harding Cox, a popular officer of the Kennel Club and author; J. Sidney Turner, president of the Kennel Club and editor of *The Kennel Encyclopædia;* Edgar Farman onetime secretary of the Kennel Club and author of that rare monument *The Bulldog;* Mrs. C. Ashton Cross so well known as author of *The Pekingese Dog;* and W. K. Taunton, C. E. Holford, Henry East, and, of course, Mrs. C. C. Edmunds—*Editor.*

Let us conclude this survey of the breed's early history with some of Somerville's wonderful lines:

> Whose ears down hanging from his thick round
> head Shall sweep the morning dew; whose clanging
> voice Awake the mountain echo in her cell,
> And shake the forests, the bold, the Talbot kind.

Or again, these most excellent passages from Whyte Melville's ' A Lay of the Ranston Bloodhounds ':

> The leaf is dead, the woods are red,
>   Autumn skies are soft and pale,
> Winds are through the copses straying,
> Ripples on the water playing.
> Hark! I hear the Bloodhound baying,
>   Down by the river in the vale!

.   .   .   .   .   .

> How the chorus pealed and gathered
>   To an organ's tone!
> How the horses steamed and lathered
>   But to hold their own!
> Like a burst of angry weather
>   In the tempest's frown,
> How the pack, at head together,
>   Swept across the down!

.   .   .   .   .   .

> Pleasure that the most enchants us,
>   Seems the soonest done;
> What is life with all it grants us,
>   But a hunting run!

CHAPTER II

CLEARLY we have seen how the Second World War brought the breed close to extinction. We contemporary breeders owe a great debt to those who continued to breed, and kept the proud heritage of our pre-war strains still going. As with several other large breeds (Mastiffs and Newfoundlands, for example) the available blood-lines were pitifully few. Outcross blood therefore became a matter of urgency, and the Association of Bloodhound Breeders decided to allow a Foxhound outcross.

I do not propose to dwell on the aspect of the post-war Foxhound outcrosses save to say that the decision to introduce them must have been a hasty one, and that I think the faults it brought to the breed far outweigh any possible good it may have done.

The decision was especially bad as pure-bred out-crosses were to become available. Fortunately some kennels, notably the 'Brighton' and the 'Barsheen', stoutly maintained their pure-bred lines, and it is these strains which, blended together with the pure-bred importations, have again brought British Bloodhounds to the fore as the world's finest type.

POST-WAR IMPORTATIONS

But for the public-spirited action of a few people Bloodhound affairs would indeed have reached a sorry pass at one stage. Then Mrs. Rosamund Oldfield and Mrs. Harris St. John imported from the U.S.A. Ch. (later International Champion) " Spotter of Littlebrook "; and Viscount and Lady Waverley (formerly Sir John and Lady Anderson) imported from Canada " Westsummerland Montgomery of Bre-Mar-Har-Ros ". And quite recently Mrs. Yvonne Oldman has imported from Mr. and Mrs. Boland of the U.S.A. the bitch " Barsheen Bynda of Huguenot ".

I now add a note on " Spotter " and " Montgomery ", and the bitch " Bynda ", and give their pedigrees.

Int. Ch. "Spotter of Littlebrook", was imported from the U.S.A. by Mrs. Rosamund Oldfield and her mother Mrs. Harris St. John at a time when currency conditions were difficult and these ladies surmounted great difficulties to get this dog to England and to make him available to British breeders.

For reasons I have never been able to understand he had a number of homes and did not appear in the show ring until he was very generously given to me. I immediately showed him and at three championship shows, under Mr. J. K. Dryden, Mr. John Beynon and Mr. Leo Wilson, he gained his international title and was never beaten in the British show ring by another dog hound. His show record in the U.S.A. was equally impressive as he had forty-one first prizes in forty-two ring appearances.

He also had in the United States a very great reputation as a man trailer having been regularly used on official business by the New Hampshire State police. For some obscure reason he never maintained his hunting prowess in this country although on the one occasion I took him to a Field Trial he did not enjoy the best of luck. His habit, as is the habit of many great hunting Bloodhounds, of hunting a line head high apparently effortlessly did not seem to appeal to many.

It was most unfortunate that in the first part of his stay here he was not in demand at stud and sired but few puppies. He met a premature death from distention at a time when breeders were enquiring for his services. What stock he left should be jealously guarded and bred from as frequently as possible. It has been suggested that " Spotter " had a difficult temperament but during his stay with me his conduct was impeccable—Mr. and Mrs. Norman of the ' Coombelane ' kennels, who were at that time managing my establishment, were sorely grieved when he died.

INT. CH. SPOTTER OF LITTLEBROOK

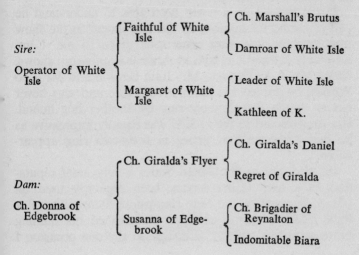

Sire:
Operator of White Isle

Faithful of White Isle
{ Ch. Marshall's Brutus
Damroar of White Isle }

Margaret of White Isle
{ Leader of White Isle
Kathleen of K. }

Dam:
Ch. Donna of Edgebrook

Ch. Giralda's Flyer
{ Ch. Giralda's Daniel
Regret of Giralda }

Susanna of Edge-brook
{ Ch. Brigadier of Reynalton
Indomitable Biara }

"**Westsummerland Mongomery of Bre-Mar-Har-Ros**". The late Lord Waverley and his wife imported this hound from Canada, again during difficult times, and again everyone should be tremendously grateful for the effort made. This hound was a red, but I personally never had the pleasure of seeing him. His detractors cannot be rude enough about his appearance but fortunately how few they are and how foolish they are. Some say he looked like a Labrador . . . well, if Bloodhounds that look like Labradors can produce such animals as Ch. "Melody of Westsummerland" and Ch. "Appeline Hector of West-summerland" my money would every time go to use such hounds.

He produced good stock; he produced virile stock, and through his son mentioned above he gave the breed tremendous depth of lip, nicely angulated shoulders, good feet and fronts and the lovely chestnut red colour.

WESTSUMMERLAND MONTGOMERY OF BRE-MAR-HAR-ROS

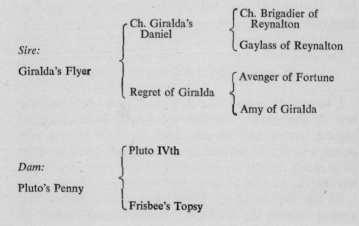

Sire:

Giralda's Flyer

Ch. Giralda's Daniel
- Ch. Brigadier of Reynalton
- Gaylass of Reynalton

Regret of Giralda
- Avenger of Fortune
- Amy of Giralda

Dam:

Pluto's Penny

- Pluto IVth
- Frisbee's Topsy

Another false charge that is laid at " Montgomery"s door is that he produces hounds with white blazes. This is completely false for the white blazes come from the Foxhound outcross, not the Canadian, and will also occasionally occur from certain English bitch lines which go back to the era of Queen Victoria and Landseer. " Montgomery " was unshown but it will be found by students of pedigrees that he now appears in the third or forth generation of a large majority of the principal winners at every championship show.

Lord and Lady Waverley were great public figures and the breed thus got very good national press publicity which was invaluable.

"Barsheen Bynda of Huguenot ". This is a black-and-tan bitch imported by Mrs. Y. Oldman a few years ago. Her outcross blood will be invaluable, though, of course, she has not yet had time to show us what qualities she can transmit. Though not a large bitch she conforms to the breed Standard, and when shown has been successfull. Fortunately she has produced her first litter in England. . . . her pedigree appears on page 18.

Bloodhounds Around the World

I have said earlier that British Bloodhounds are the best in the world, and that the breed has reached its highest quality and modern form in these islands, but perhaps as far as usefulness is concerned it has reached its greatest development in the U.S.A., where the breed has been known for at least a century.

At the time when the abolitionists were campaigning against slavery heart-rending pictures were drawn of

BARSHEEN BYNDA OF HUGUENOT

Sire: Am. Ch. Essex Fancy Thomas	Am. Ch. Fancy Bombardier	Trooper of White Isle
		Am. Ch. Rumpus of Folsom
	Roger's Fancy Investigator	Bozo of Ramapo
		Am. Ch. Fancy of Point O'Forks
Dam: Sheba's Renee Fischer	Am. Ch. Rye of Panther Ledge	Am. Ch. Giralda's Kriss
		Am. Ch. Wuthering Tiny of Brighton
	Renee's Sheba	Trooper of White Isle
		Am. Ch. Fancy of Point O'Forks

fugitive slaves being pursued by Bloodhounds, but it is
doubtful if these particular hounds were pure bred.
Where it has been necessary for the hounds to attack and
hold the fugitives rather than seek and safely identify
them various types of crossing has been used, but many
spectacular arrests have been recorded by pure-bred
hounds. Bloodhounds have been widely used in the
U.S.A. by the owners of southern plantations, prison
authorities, sheriffs and policemen. Probably the greatest of these was " Nick Carter " (see Plate VII), a hound
who accounted for over 600 finds. Capt. V. G. Mullikin
was probably the greatest American man hunter and over
2,500 finds and convictions resulted from his activities.

Plate I

'Bloodhound on the Trail', by Reinagle, 1820.

Canis Dog Features.

odhounds' by
enham Teak
Edwards, 1800.

Canis Dog Features.

'Bloodhounds on the Trail', by C. B. Goddard, 1878.

Canis Dog Features.

Plate II

Canis Dog Features.

Sir Edwin Landseer's ' Sleeping Bloodhound '
(Jacob Bell's " Countess "), 1835.

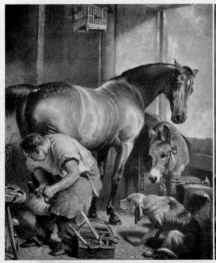

Canis Dog Features.

Sir Edwin Landseer's ' Shoeing the Bay
Mare ' (with " Laura "), 1844.

Canis Dog Feat

Sir Edwin Landseer's ' Dignity
Impudence ' (with " Grafton "), 1

He often charged a fee for his work and the largest recorded that he received is 5,000 dollars. Other great man hunters of the New World include the famous cynologist Leon Whitney, Dr. Jenkins, Will Thomas, ' Cy ' Houghton, and troopers Brown and Anderson.

The Bloodhound has also received considerable support from American exhibitors; the hounds of Mrs. Geraldine R. Dodge (' Giralda '), Bob and Mary Lees Noerr ('The Ring '), editor of the *Bloodhound Breeders' Bulletin*, Mr. and Mrs. Boland (' Huguenot '), Mrs. Ryan (' Panther Ledge '), and others are known all over the world.

I am frequently asked how British hounds compare with those in the United States. The American hounds are very often professionally handled and somehow the hounds are brought into the ring in much smarter coat condition with cleaner outlines. This may be the result of hard work or it may be due to artificial aids. Watching American hounds being judged one can get the impression that soundness is given too much emphasis over type. British hounds score over the Americans very heavily in head and ears, feet, bone and loose skin. They are also a little better in depth of body and strength of quarters.

In Norway and Sweden dual purpose hounds are quite well known and the principal breeder is Sergeant Erik Pettersson, who exhibits at shows and trains hounds for the Swedish police forces. In Denmark there is Mr. Poul Lassen who has just embarked on a breeding programme with a bitch he imported from Britain.

Mrs. S. K. Mitra of Calcutta most certainly keeps the breed alive at her celebrated ' Hundezuchter ' variety kennels in India and has had several Best in Show wins with her imported hounds. And Mr. B. F. N. Arnolda

c

combines show ring activities with wild boar hunting for his Bloodhounds in Ceylon.

Mr. Douglas Henderson of the 'Winsace' kennels, Brisbane, Australia, has been breeding Bloodhounds since 1946 but has recently had difficulties owing to the shortage of fresh blood—however, Mr. Douglas Mummery of Victoria has recently paid a visit to England and purchased several hounds which he has shipped to his own country. These hounds are to form the nucleus of a breeding programme and are to be trained for police work in Australia.

At the fine dog shows in Spain and along the Mediterranean coasts the hounds of Mr. Martinez are exhibited, whilst in France the hounds of Mme. Anne Besson are frequently seen on the show bench.

In Holland Mr. Jos Gillissen is Master of the Hubertus Hunt, a pack of pure-bred Bloodhounds hunting fox. The hounds are kennelled at 'de St. Hubertushof', Leusden (U), Holland (see Plate XIII).

To return home for a moment I should add that in Scotland Sir John Buchanan-Jardine, Bart, M.C., and Major R. Buchanan-Jardine hunt the Dumfriesshire Foxhounds, but this pack is most unusual as all the hounds carry Bloodhound blood, and all forty couples are black-and-tan. Sir John is the author of that excellent work *Hounds of the World*, 1937, which is still one of the finest books on French breed of hounds.

POPULARISING THE BREED

The contemporary Bloodhound is safe from extinction but even so we have absolutely no room for complacency. During my travels I am frequently asked what can be done, or what is needed, to widen interest in the breed.

The answers to this question are simple:

1. The breed should be promoted as a companion dog to the type of household where he can fit in as part of the family unit.

2. At dog shows Bloodhound exhibitors should encourage other fanciers to take up the breed.

3. Police forces should be encouraged to keep some Bloodhounds on their official dog strength.

The achievement of these points however is not so simple but they are only capable of solution if the larger breeders really help and everyone acts with complete integrity.

To ensure a good and continuous pet market temperament is of paramount importance, no dog or bitch should be bred from, however good the show points, unless it is completely good natured under all circumstances. People wanting a Bloodhound puppy should be encouraged to take him as young as possible—an intelligent owner can quite successfully cope with a puppy of six or seven weeks of age. For the pet owner elaborate feeding charts are frightening and I know of people turning to other breeds because they have been scared off when presented with an unnecessarily elaborate feeding schedule. The busy housewife to whose lot it nearly always falls to rear the pup just has not the time to give the eight meals a day which are often recommended. While this mass of meals makes for quicker early growth it produces fussy feeders and no increase in ultimate size. Four meals daily, reducing to one at twelve months of age are quite adequate.

Show exhibitors will not take up a new breed unless they see some chance of getting their noses in and doing some winning, and it is therefore necessary that the ownership of the best hounds should be more widely spread. It is also a great help to a particular variety of exhibitors in other breeds if they see that a happy and congenial atmosphere prevails before and after judging, as few people want to join a disgruntled band of people.

I can never understand the philosophy of a breeder who fears selling a good hound in case he beats their own in the ring. It is a far greater boost for a kennel to have *bred and sold* a Champion than it is to own one. It is always essential that a puppy sold as a show prospect should in fact be one and in this breed it is very easy to sort out the geese from the swans early on— good rearing will do the rest.

The American police use Bloodhounds in large numbers. The Australian, Canadian and Swedish police forces are using them in increasing numbers too, yet our own authorities just do not seem to be interested in giving the breed a serious trial. I feel sure if those in charge of police dog organizations in Britain would, if they investigated the matter with open minds and subsequently gave Bloodhounds a fair trial, find them a most satisfactory aid to their organizations. Alsatians, Labradors and Dobermann Pinchers are widely used yet none of these has scenting power in any measure comparable to that of a good Bloodhound.

At this stage let us consider some facts and fallacies. The Bloodhound is *not* a bloodthirsty creature; nor is he able to voluntarily oblige as a blood donor, as demanded by that very funny man Benny Hill, who when introducing Ch. " Hector " to his co-star Belinda Lee, requested " Hector, bleed for the lady "!

The breed is synonymous with the solution of crime but the hounds do not make deductions, they follow carefully and relentlessly the trials on which they are started. To some degree any cur dog can follow the scent of man and even the hounds which hunt by sight can follow the hot trail of someone they know well. My coursing Greyhounds will often slope off noses down after some member of the household who has gone for a stroll.

Film and television studios make frequent use of the breed for both humorous and dramatic sequences. The hounds are quick to learn and temperamentally suited for the job but strong studio lighting seems to make it hard for most hounds to see. Unfortunately few directors allow the hounds to follow a trail in the proper way but usually insist on hounds being in couples dragging the handler behind in a manner completely impracticable during a real job of work.

RECORDS

Various works to which I have had access would indicate that the following are records in size and achievement.

Head—the longest were the fourteen inches of the American dog " Crusader ", and the English hound " Barsheen Hurryon " (Ch. " Barsheen Gem ", by Ch. "Appeline Hector of Westsummerland ").

Ear Span—thirty-three inches.

Height to shoulder—thirty-one and a half inches.

Weight—one hundred and fifty-five pounds.

Longest successful trail—fifty-five miles (handler Capt. V. G. Mullikin of the U.S.A.).

Oldest trail—three hundred and thirty-seven hours cold. (Oregon, Canada.)

Greatest number of C.Cs.—Hylden's Ch. " Dark of Brighton ", winner of thirty-one.

Maximum Best in Show wins—American Ch. " Fancy Bombardier ".

Largest litter—sixteen live puppies.

Longest pregnancy—one live puppy delivered after seventy-two days.

GOVERNING BODIES

Dog breeding and showing in Britain is governed by the Kennel Club. Its objects are to promote the improvement of dogs, dog shows and Field Trials, and: ' include the classification of breeds, the registration of pedigrees, transfers, etc., the license of shows and the framing and enforcing of Kennel Club rules, the awarding of challenge and champion certificates, the registration of associations, clubs and societies, and the publication of an annual Stud Book and a monthly Kennel Gazette.'

The **Kennel Club**, whose present patron is Her Majesty Queen Elizabeth, was founded in 1873 and deals with the registration and recording of Bloodhound pedigrees, the control of all shows, the approval of judges at championship shows and Working Trials. Without its wisdom dog breeding and showing would become a badly disorganized, muddled business. The present secretary is Mr. E. Holland Buckley. The interests of both the show bench hounds and the Field Trialers are cared for by this body.

Bloodhounds cannot be exhibited at a Kennel Club show, or entered in a Working Trial unless they are registered with the Kennel Club. The Show and Working Trial Rules and Regulations enforced by the Kennel Club are given in later chapters, and operating under the auspices of this body are the Association of Bloodhound Breeders and the Bloodhound Club.

The functions and objects of these clubs are similar. They look after the general interests of the breed, assist dog show societies by guaranteeing classes and giving trophies and cash prizes and in making every effort to see that hounds are given the opportunity to hunt man. With this latter object in view, Field Trials are organized. Membership of these clubs costs, at present, one guinea per annum and those interested in the breed should consider the advantages offered by membership.

The Association of Bloodhound Breeders, was founded in 1897 and as a result of the hard work of the honorary secretary, Mrs. Langdale of Levant Park Farm, Chichester, Sussex, is thriving and active. At first Trials were held on short hot lines but later became ambitious enough to reach present-day conditions.

It is interesting to note that in the early days members had to contribute ten per cent of all prize monies won at Working Trials and shows, in addition to the annual subscription which, even then, was one guinea. Membership of the Association must therefore be one of the very few things that costs less to-day than it did sixty years ago, for the donation of a percentage of prize money is no longer enforced.

The Bloodhound Club, which began as the Bloodhound Hunt Club, is some five or six years the junior,
being founded by some leading fanciers in 1903. It
was temporarily in the doldrums after the death of the
secretary, Mrs. N. E. Elms, but Mr. Alan Brews kept
the finances in good order. The Club is now making
sound progress under the presidency of the Viscount
Chelmsford and the chairmanship of Mr. R. S. Townson.
The present secretary is Mr. D. H. Appleton, of Green
Keys Farm, Oulton, Norwich.

This latter club offers without charge to its members
the advantage of a third party insurance scheme whereby
if the hound causes damage to person or property the
owner is fully covered by a policy which gives indemnity
up to £25,000 for each and every claim plus legal costs
incurred with the concurrence of the insurers. It also
covers legal costs of defence of proceedings under the
Dogs (Protection of Livestock) Act, 1953.

Earlier founders of the Club included such famous
names as Mrs. G. A. J. Oliphant, Mr. Henry East and
Mr. H. Stocker, while the first president was the Earl
of Cardigan.

In the U.S.A. the **American Kennel Club** of 221,
Fourth Avenue, New York, 3, governs the canine world,
and the breed club is the **American Bloodhound Club**,
This club operates on a similar basis to the British clubs,
supports shows, organizes Field Trials and hound training afternoons. It publishes in addition a quarterly
bulletin giving up-to-date information of the breed in
that country, together with helpful articles of general
interest.

The honorary secretary of this club is Mr. A. Kent
McClelland of 88, Second Street, Garden City, New

York. The president is Mr. Robert V. Lindsay of R.F.D.I., Steward Lane, Syosset, New York.

Before dealing with the breed Standard here is a list of the holders of some of the best known Bloodhound affixes (mainly British). These are placed in alphabetical order for easy reference, and although the breeders listed are not all still with us the kennel names will long be found in Bloodhound pedigrees.

LEADING KENNELS

Almscliffe	Mrs. M. C. Oldfield
Ambleow	Miss J. Quarmby
Annmere	Mr. G. R. Stephenson
Appeline	Mr. D. H. Appleton
Barchester	Mrs. M. Sadleir
Barsheen	Mrs. Y. Oldman
Benjairg	Mrs. G. A. Woodall
Brighton	Mr. F. and Miss L. V. Hylden
Brundish	Mrs. G. N. H. Hayes
Buxhall	Mrs. P. Allington
Carrigmore	Mrs. G. Volpe
Donimay	Mr. D. E. Rook
Duplex	Mrs. E. Lennie
Easebourne	Mr. and Mrs. A. M. Langdale
Feolin	Miss P. Redman
Fredwell	Mrs. J. Wells
Gordonstoun	Gordonstoun School
Hellidon	Mrs. J. H. Moor
Huguenot	Mrs. G. W. Boland (U.S.A.)
Hurstwood	Mrs. D. W. Basset
Kelperland	Mr. R. S. Townson
Killandini	Viscountess Portman
Kimstowe	Mr. V. Hutchings
Kirtle	Hon. Lady Johnson-Ferguson
Lakespark	Dr. F. T. Madge
Marlwood	Mr. J. E. M. Mellor
Metesford	Mrs. W. Halstead

Monksbrow	Mrs. L. M. Whiting
Neilworth	Mrs. J. H. Neil
Nenthorn	Mrs. D. R. Thomson
Northanger	Mrs. L. Valentine
Podlea	Mrs. D. Hull
Raycroft	Mr. and Mrs. C. E. Furness
Reynalton	Mrs. N. E. Elms
Rytow	Mr. R. Wright
Sansome	Mrs. R. M. Cole
The Ring	Mr. and Mrs. R. E. Noerr (U.S.A.)
Thunderdell	Mrs. F. M. Scott
Westsummerland ...	Viscountess Waverley
Winsace	Mr. D. Henderson
Woodcote	Mr. and Mrs. J. W. G. Crocker
Wuthering	Mrs. M. C. Oldfield and Mr. C. S. Nicholls
Wylmington	Mrs. K. Halswell

CHAPTER III

By courtesy of the Kennel Club

Characteristics—The Bloodhound possesses, in a most marked degree, every point and characteristic of those dogs which hunt together by scent (*Sagaces*). He is very powerful, and stands over more ground than is usual with hounds of other breeds. The skin is thin to the touch and extremely loose, this being more especially noticeable about the head and neck, where it hangs in deep folds. In temperament he is extremely affectionate, neither quarrelsome with companions nor with other dogs. His nature is somewhat shy, and equally sensitive to kindness or correction by his master.

General Appearance—The expression is noble and dignified, and characterised by solemnity, wisdom and power. The gait is elastic swinging and free, the stern being carried high, but not too much curled over the back.

Head and Skull—The head is narrow in proportion to its length and long in proportion to the body, tapering but slightly from the temples to the end of the muzzle, thus (when viewed from above and in front) having the appearance of being flattened at the sides and of being nearly equal in width throughout its entire length. In profile the upper outline of the skull is nearly in the same plane as that of the foreface. The length from the end of nose to stop (midway between the eyes) should be not less than that from stop to back of occipital protuberance (peak). The entire length of head from the posterior part of the occipital protuberance to the end of the muzzle should be 12 inches or more in dogs, and 11 inches or more in bitches. The skull is long and narrow, with the occipital peak very pronounced. The brows are not prominent, although owing to the deep-set eyes they may have that appearance. The foreface is long, deep, and of even width throughout, with square outline when seen in profile. The head is furnished with an amount of loose skin, which in nearly every position appears super-abundant, but more particularly so when the head is carried low; the skin then falls into loose, pendulous ridges and folds, especially over the forehead and sides of the face. The nostrils are large and open. In front the lips fall squarely, making a right-angle with the upper line of the foreface; whilst behind they form deep, hanging flews, and, being continued into the pendant folds of loose skin about the neck, constitute the dewlap, which is very pronounced. These characters are found, though in a less degree, in the bitch.

Eyes—The eyes are deeply sunk in the orbits, the lids assuming a lozenge or diamond shape, in consequence of the lower lids being dragged down and everted by the heavy flews. The eyes correspond with the general tone of colour of the animal, varying from deep hazel to yellow. The hazel colour is, however, to be preferred, although very seldom seen in the red-and-tan hounds.

Ears—The ears are thin and soft to the touch, extremely long, set very low, and fall in graceful folds, the lower parts curling inwards and backwards.

Neck—Should be long.

Forequarters—The shoulders muscular and well sloped backwards. The forelegs are straight and large in bone, with elbows squarely set.

Body—The ribs are well sprung; and the chest well let down between the forelegs, forming a deep keel. The back and loins are strong, the latter deep and slightly arched.

Hindquarters—The thighs and second thighs (gaskins) are very muscular, the hocks well bent and let down, and squarely set.

Feet—Should be strong and well knuckled up.

Tail—The tail is long and tapering, and set on rather high, with a moderate amount of hair underneath.

Colour—The colours are black-and-tan, red-and-tan, and tawny; the darker colours being sometimes interspersed with lighter or badger coloured hair, and sometimes flecked with white. A small amount of white is permissible on chest, feet and tip of stern.

Weight and Size—The mean average height of adult dogs is 26 inches and of bitches 24 inches. Dogs usually vary from 25 to 27 in. and bitches from 23 to 25 in., but in either case the greater height is to be preferred, provided that the character and quality are also combined. The mean average weight of adult dogs, in fair condition is 90lb., and of adult bitches 80lb. Dogs attain the weight of 110lb., bitches 100lb. The greater weights are to be preferred, provided (as in the case of height) that quality and proportion are also combined.

AMERICAN STANDARD

(By courtesy of the American Kennel Club)

General Character—The Bloodhound possesses, in a most marked degree, every point and characteristic of those dogs which hunt together by scent (*Sagaces*). He is very powerful, and stands over more ground than is usual with hounds of other breeds. The skin is thin to the touch and extremely loose, this being more especially noticeable about the head and neck, where it hangs in deep folds.

Height—The mean average height of adult dogs is 26 inches, and of adult bitches 24 inches. Dogs usually vary from 25 inches to 27 inches, and bitches from 23 inches to 25 inches; but, in either case the greater height is to be preferred, provided that character and quality are also combined.

Weight—The mean average weight of adult dogs, in fair condition, is 90 pounds, and of adult bitches 80 pounds. Dogs attain the weight of 110 pounds, bitches 100 pounds. The greater weights are to be preferred, provided (as in the case of height) that quality and proportion are also combined.

Expression—The expression is noble and dignified, and characterized by solemnity, wisdom and power.

Temperament—In temperament he is extremely affectionate, neither quarrelsome with companions nor with other dogs. His nature is somewhat shy, and equally sensitive to kindness or correction by his master.

Head—The head is narrow in proportion to its length and long in proportion to the body, tapering but slightly from the temples to the end of the muzzle, thus (when viewed from above and in front) having the appearance of being flattened at the sides and of being nearly equal in width throughout its entire length. In profile the upper outline of the skull is nearly in the same plane as that of the foreface. The length from end of nose to stop (midway between the eyes) should be not less than that from stop to back of occipital protuberance (peak). The entire length of head from the posterior part of the occipital protuberance to the end of the muzzle should be 12 inches, or more, in dogs, and 11 inches, or more, in bitches.

Skull—The skull is long and narrow, with the occipital peak very pronounced. The brows are not prominent, although, owing to the deep-set eyes, they may have that appearance.

Foreface—The foreface is long, deep, and of even width throughout, with square outline when seen in profile.

Eyes—The eyes are deeply sunk in the orbits, the lids assuming a lozenge or diamond shape, in consequence of the lower lids being dragged down and everted by the heavy flews. The eyes correspond with the general tone of colour of the animal, varying from deep hazel to yellow. The hazel colour is, however, to be preferred, although very seldom seen in red-and-tan hounds.

Ears—The ears are thin and soft to the touch, extremely long, set very low, and fall in graceful folds, the lower parts curling inwards and backwards.

Wrinkle—The head is furnished with an amount of loose skin, which in nearly every position appears superabundant, but more particularly so when the head is carried low; the skin then falls into loose, pendulous ridges and folds, especially over the forehead and sides of the face.

Nostrils—The nostrils are large and open.

Lips, Flews and Dewlap—In front the lips fall squarely, making a right-angle with the upper line of the foreface; whilst behind they form deep hanging flews, and, being continued into the pendant folds of loose skin about the neck, constitute the dewlap, which is very pronounced. These characters are found, though in a less degree, in the bitch.

Neck, Shoulders and Chest—The neck is long, the shoulders muscular and well sloped backwards; the

Plate III

Briton Riviére's ' Last of the Garrison ', 1875.

Riviére's ' In Manus Tua Domine ', 1879.

Plate IV

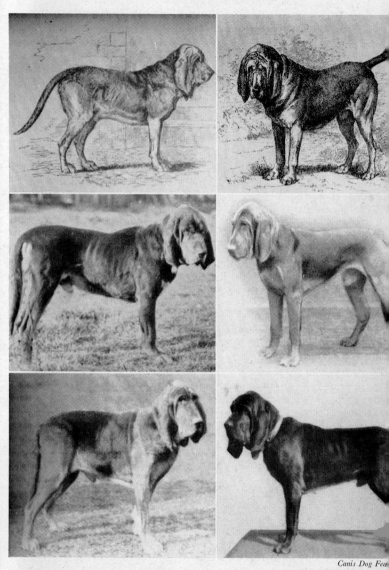

Canis Dog Fea

Six famous early Hounds (*left to right*) : Rev. G. Straton's " Luath XI " ; G. R. K
Ch. " Cromwell " ; H. G. H. Sandeman's Ch. " Blazer " ; E. Brough's " Burgun
E. Brough's Ch. " Barbarossa " ; A. Croxton Smith's " Panther ".

ribs are well sprung; and the chest well let down
between the forelegs, forming a deep keel.

Legs and Feet—The forelegs are straight and large in
bone, with elbows squarely set; the feet strong and
well knuckled up; the thighs and second thighs
(gaskins) are very muscular; the hocks well bent
and let down, and squarely set.

Back and Loin—The back and loins are strong, the
latter deep and slightly arched.

Stern—The stern is long and tapering, and set on rather
high, with a moderate amount of hair underneath.

Gait—The gait is elastic, swinging and free, the stern
being carried high, but not too much curled over
the back.

Colour—The colours are black-and-tan, red-and-tan,
and tawny; the darker colours being sometimes
interspersed with lighter or badger coloured hair,
and sometimes flecked with white. A small amount
of white is permissible on chest, feet, and tip of
stern.

ANALYSIS

The Bloodhound Standard, included in this chapter, outlines the essential physical characteristics of the
breed. A hound conforming strictly to this Standard
will, if he has the unseen hunting qualities, be able to
do his job far better than a hound who possesses the
unseen qualities but lacks physical perfection.

D

It is complete and utter nonsense to decry the good that dog shows do. In obedience competitions and in Field Trials, we see to-day animals working that have no resemblance to the breed they claim to represent. Some so-called Alsatians look more like Collies, and some so-called Setters resemble I know not what, but certainly not Setters. It is as bad for a working dog or hound to be just a shadow of the breed he represents as it is for the show dog to become over exaggerated to suit the whims of show bench specialists. The aim of everyone in every working breed should be to produce the dual purpose animal.

The breed Standard we are discussing was drawn up by people who were interested in the Bloodhound as a man trailer just as much as they were interested in it as a show bench hound. The Standard has stood the test of time and is a good one. It could, however, be improved by the addition of a description of the serious and minor faults.

Such a Standard is subject to varied interpretations but the fundamentals will always be the same. If a fixed interpretation were possible or applicable there would be scant point in having shows as the same hounds would nearly always win.

It is this varied interpretation that makes dog showing interesting. The learned gentlemen with a deeply scientific approach sometimes tell us that it is possible for the good looking animals to be produced with certainty in every litter. However, these folk do not seem able to fill the show ring with their successes.

All who judge or breed hounds should study and evaluate what a hound has to do during a long hunt, and matings should be planned to breed hounds able to cope with the job. A job which calls for the ability to

gallop fast and tirelessly when the scent is breast high—
to plod on carefully and painstakingly with no loss of
concentration when scent is patchy—to swim a stream—-
to jump a ditch—or to scale a wall. These things the
hound must be able to do in a tropical heat or with ice
underfoot.

When evaluating a hound the first requirement must
be for *type*—overall and balanced Bloodhound type—
the animal must look *all* Bloodhound. It is no use having a wonderful head for the breed if it is set on a Greyhound body, or a body of size quality and substance
surmounted by the head of a Foxhound.

The next consideration is soundness. Some may say
that soundness is more important than type but even in
a working breed type must come first.

MOVEMENT

When assessing soundness in the show ring a judge can
only assume from conformation the galloping abilities of
a hound, but he can judge movement in the slower paces.
Movement should be fluid and free and an enormous
amount of ground should be covered. The correctly
made hound will always move well and when the
knowledgable judge asks for an exhibit to be moved he
will, in practically every case, only demonstrate to him
the quality of movement that has been suggested by the
bone structure. Movement must be assessed 'going
away ', ' coming to ', and from the side view.

Going away the legs should move parallel with
smoothness and drive, and give an indication of a reserve
of the power needed when he has to gallop. There must
be no sign of cow hocks, an overwide hind action or

of the insides of the rear feet coming close together.

Coming to you the front legs must remain parallel and the feet must be lifted clear of the ground but not so high as to give a hackney action. Movement must not cause the frame to roll though it will of course cause suggestion of roll through the flexibility of loose skin. The front feet must not come together in a paddling action, neither must there be any looseness or coming out at the elbows.

Side view the stride must be free, flowing and effort-less, showing good coverage of the ground with the ability to ' eat it up ' and with every indication of having immense reserves of power. Such movement is possible because the shoulders, elbows, hips and stifles are correctly placed and angulated, and free movement under the chest and loins is possible. A sound Blood-hound must, like a good horse, move on the proper lead.

There must be no suggestion of the action being short, rough or choppy. When in movement the stern should be carried in the air showing a confident demean-our. All lack of breed type and incorrect movement are serious faults.

BREED POINTS

As we come to consider various points of the hound we find some faults are serious, some not so serious and some minor. And as we discuss these, to indicate their importance, after each fault will appear (A) for serious, (B) for the not so serious and (C) for the minor ones.

Temperament must be taken into account when judg-ing; a hound who is nervous (A) or vicious (A) must be penalized. While the Standard says ' his nature is shy ' it does not mean nervous but rather that the hound is sufficient unto himself until he knows you.

Under ' General Appearance ' our previous considerations on type have dealt with all the points made except for a description of the stern and position of carriage. This must be carried high, almost like a scimitar, set on fairly high with a thick root. And while the Standard calls for the stern to be ' long ' it does not mean too long (B): it must balance the hound. A hound who moves with stern right down (A) or who carries it curled to the back (A) should be penalized. This latter fault invariably goes with faulty hind movement (A).

The head and skull is amply detailed needing very little further comment. Some coarseness or greater width in the skull (marked (C) for dogs and (B) for bitches) is frequently seen and is not too incorrect—in fact one or two of our specialist judges like to see it. The section reading ' with square outline when seen in profile ' is most important, for too many hounds, especially dog hounds, have been short of lip (A). It is a strongly hereditary fault and the fact that it is now less widespread is due to the importation from Canada of " Westsummerland Montgomery of Bre-Mar-Har-Ros ".

Head lengths should certainly not be much less (A) than that given in the Standard and the longer the better, providing there is sufficient lip. Ample natural wrinkle is most important—I say natural wrinkle as any hound will show wrinkle if the handler pulls down loose skin and holds it in position. The specification of ' nostrils are large and open ' is too often disregarded. Small tight nostrils (A) make it difficult for a hound to do his job.

The teeth should be even, white and strong with a scissor bite. An undershot (B) or an overshot mouth (B) must be faulted as must dirty or bad teeth (C), although these latter are to be blamed on the owner unless they are distemper teeth.

The eyes have been discussed under breed problems. An eye that has been operated on (B) should be faulted as should an eye damaged (A) through lack of treatment. A genuine hunting injury to the eye should be forgiven, as in fact, should any hunting scars. At present the bold eye (C) must be penalized. The Standard states that a yellow eye is permissible but that hazel is to be preferred. However, colour has improved so much that light eyes (B) deserve some penalty. The red hounds now often have a darker eye than the black-and-tans. This improvement in the eye colour of the reds is due to the imported blood.

The ears must be thin to the touch—a thick ear (C) does not hang quite so gracefully. A short ear (A) entirely spoils the head, as does a high set ear (B). Set on very low means that the ear must join the head below an imaginary line drawn back from the eye, parallel to the muzzle when the top of this is held parallel to the ground.

Length of neck is called for, and this ensures that a hound easily gets his head down to work. Short stuffy necks (B) go with bad shoulders. When a hound has really abundant loose skin this sometimes gives the false impression that the neck lacks length so physical examination is necessary.

The shoulders must be well laid otherwise a hound takes too much out of himself when he gallops. Straight shoulders (A) are bad. Forelegs must be straight. Crooked bone (A), weak pasterns (B) or deficiency of bone (A) are one of the faults resulting from bad rearing.

A hound must not be out at the elbows (B). The construction of the body must show immense strength. Ribs must be clean and strong. The brisket should come some three inches below the elbows and the chest should be very well rounded. It should also be noted that, lack of depth of body (A) and slab sides (A) do not allow the essential room for heart and lungs. Back must be level and loins very strong, not ultra short (C) nor over long (B). A dip in the back (B) is a weakness.

Hindquarters must be well muscled and powerful. Lack of muscle (B), cow hocks (A) and straight stifles (A) are faults.

Feet—Oh, these feet! they are the whole mounting on which the hound stands and take him about his daily work, yet they are so often neglected—too frequently excused. I have said, and to stress it, say again, that good feet are bred and not made. However, good feet can be spoiled by neglect. Long nails (B)—there is no excuse for these. Paper feet (A), badly knuckled feet (A) are all too frequently seen. Paper feet are a fault often observed in the United States.

The colours given in the Standard are easy to understand but the problem comes when it has to be decided how much white is permissible. Some white on the chest, let us say up to an area that can be covered by both hands, is acceptable, as are some white toes. White socks (B) and a larger amount of white on the chest (C) must incur some penalty. Now for consideration of the white blaze—a blaze such as seen on a St. Bernard (A) or in some early engravings of Bloodhounds must be clamped down upon but too many specialists condemn a hound for a few white hairs (C) on the muzzle or brow— and this is taking specialization too far. It is undoubtedly a fault and must be penalized, but never to the extent that a bad mouth or bad feet should be.

Much of the white seen in the breed to-day is due to the Foxhound outcross. Some of it has been blamed on the Canadian influence but this is a false charge. Bitches when mated to hounds containing Canadian blood have produced whelps with white blazes but the same bitches, when mated to 100% British hounds have again produced whelps with the same fault, while an experimental heavy inbreeding to the Canadian outcross produced a litter with virtually no white at all.

The whole body of the hound should be abundantly covered with loose skin; one definition is that this loose skin should be thin to the touch but flexible is probably a better term. This loose skin is really a most important breed feature and hounds without it over the body quite naturally also lack sufficient wrinkle on the head. A Bloodhound is called upon to do his job whatever the weather and coat texture is also important if he is to receive adequate protection. A correct coat texture is one that is dense and smooth but not too short; a fine seal coat looks very nice but does not keep out the wet and cold, and a coarse harsh coat is not dense enough to stop wet penetrating it.

Measurements

The (A), (B) and (C) evaluation I give on faults is intended only as a rough guide to the novice and not as an absolutely rigid yardstick. The following comparison of measurements of three well-known hounds is of great interest. The hounds compared are:

1. Champion "Don", bred in 1875 and universally recognized by old-time judges as the greatest of his era.
2. Mrs. R. A. Oldfield and Mr. C. S. Nichol's Champion "Dasher of Brighton", the only post-war Bloodhound to be Best in Show all breeds at a championship show.
3. Champion "Appeline Hector of Westsummerland", winner of four Challenge Certificates and one of the most successful of the contemporary sires.

	1	2	3
Tip of nose to stop	5 in.	6¼ in.	5¼ in.
Stop to occiput	8 in.	6½ in.	7¾ in.
Total length of head	13 in.	12¾ in.	13 in.
Length of back	29 in.	24 in.	25 in.
Girth of muzzle	14 in.	14 in.	13½ in.
Girth of skull	21½ in.	22 in.	20½ in.
Girth of neck	24 in.	24 in.	23 in.
Girth round brisket	38 in.	38 in.	38½ in.
Girth round chest	35 in.	39 in.	33 in.
Girth of loins	29¾ in.	30 in.	29 in.
Girth of thigh	18 in.	19 in.	18 in.
Girth of forearm	8¾ in.	9 in.	9 in.
Girth of pastern	5¼ in.	6 in.	5½ in.
Height at shoulders	28 in.	28 in.	28 in.
Height at elbows	15 in.	15¼ in.	15 in.
Length of stern	18 in.	19 in.	18 in.
Weight	99 lb.	101 lb.	105 lb.

Illustrations show that the breed has altered little during the last hundred years and the foregoing figures showing Ch. "Don" of some eighty-four years ago, Ch. "Dasher" of ten years ago and Ch. "Hector" of to-day as they compare each with the other prove a fascinating comparison, and that hounds have also altered little in size.

The greatest post-war change would appear to be that hounds have straighter boned front legs.

JUDGES

The selection of judges for this or any breed is always a difficult and sometimes controversial problem. The present system whereby the shows regulations committee of the Kennel Club has the final word in the selection of judges to award Challenge Certificates on the whole works very well and it is up to the breed clubs to ensure that a sufficient number of people are enabled to gain experience at the smaller events so they can eventually be selected to award C.Cs. A common complaint is the shortage of new faces amongst judges but when the choice of a judge for a small event comes up for discussion exhibitors refuse to support a newcomer and plump for an established championship show judge.

In this breed, and again as in many others, a few kennels frequently gain the major awards. When the selection of judges comes up for consideration I feel most strongly that the owners of these kennels should discreetly avoid expressing a viewpoint for while they continue to have the best stock and are likely to win it creates a nicer atmosphere all round if they let others choose the judges. The judges' verdict should, as often as is humanly possible, be right—it is almost as important that it should also look right.

The most successful breeders and exhibitors do not always make the best judges as occasionally they are so prejudiced against a single fault that they cannot produce a balanced judgment on the hound as a whole. In a breed such as Bloodhounds I feel a correct balance would be struck at championship shows if 60% of the judges were all-rounders and 40% specialists.

CHAPTER IV

THE PET BLOODHOUND

FREQUENTLY I am asked if Bloodhounds make good pets —well the answer is a definite ' Yes '.

Throughout its history the breed has been noted for its good temperament. Let me quote the views on this point of several well-known authorities:

RAWDON B. LEE wrote: '. . . . he has always had admirers who kept him for his own sake—because of his handsome and noble appearance and because he was faithful and affectionate '.

A. CROXTON SMITH: ' In disposition he is docile and affectionate '. . . . and ' Aristocratic in appearance, they are nature's gentlemen '.

G. A. J. OLIPHANT and M. E. K. OLIPHANT: ' The Bloodhound is easily broken from running stock or game and makes an excellent companion; he is not a fighter, is easily trained to the house; no dog is more amenable to kindness, less likely to forget an old friend or to resent ill treatment or injury '.

F. C. HARRISON: ' There is no doubt that they have a most kindly disposition and are entirely safe with children. They are easily house-trained and their behaviour leaves nothing to be desired '.

LEON F. WHITNEY (author of *Bloodhounds and How to Train Them*): '. . . . a Bloodhound is mild and gentle'.

While WHYTE MELVILLE wrote of their voices: 'Full, sonorous and musical, it is not extravagant to compare these deep-mouthed notes with the peal of an organ in a cathedral'.

And there the case for the Bloodhound as a pet rests. He offers all the virtues and, if you want, even cathedral music for the asking! The remaining question is ' Can such a hound fit into a small flat or house? '—well, a dog of any size can and will, for whatever his surroundings he is happy so long as he is by his master's side.

Bloodhounds as domestic pets can make wonderful additions to the family circle. True they are hounds of substance but when one considers the standard height to the top of the shoulders which is 23—27 inches it will be appreciated that they are no larger than many of the breeds which enjoy great domestic popularity.

The coat needs little attention and the allegation that Bloodhounds give off an objectionable odour is completely false. A dirty hound of any variety will smell objectionable—as indeed do dirty members of the human race. The feet are tight and well knuckled up, so they do not bring a lot of dirt into the house even on the muckiest of days. Those who have known the gentleness, loyalty and affection of these hounds have enjoyed one of life's greatest experiences, and will seldom turn to another breed. And while as a general rule Bloodhound temperament is not such that they can be labelled 'good guard dogs' but their appearance invariably acts as a strong deterrent to unlawful intruders.

I would most strongly recommend however that the pet hound should never *never* be used at stud, because the emotions aroused in a hound can greatly unsettle his temperament, and at least will make him love his home less and take himself off in search of a girl friend. A young hound may go through a period of being sexy but he will quickly grow out of this and, as with most things in life, what one has never had one does not greatly miss. But there is absolutely no reason at all why the pet bitch should not be bred from, and in fact her health in later life will benefit if she has a litter.

Finally on the sex question in relation to hounds I would most strongly advise against a bitch being spayed and even more strongly against a dog being castrated. This latter procedure is utterly wrong whatever the circumstances in a dog of any breed and can turn a pleasant animal into a sly, unreliable vicious creature. I am sure it is only those people with very limited experience of dogs who ever recommend such a foolhardy operation.

Elsewhere we shall discuss some problems in relation to the breed but the fact that these problems exist should not deter you if you desire to have a pet Bloodhound or for that matter if a kennel wishes to add them as another string.

The adult hound for his size eats surprisingly little for they are not greedy dogs and their placid nature prevents them from wasting vast amounts of energy and thus promoting appetite.

Your hound may have been purchased solely as a companion, as a hound to hunt, or as a guard, but whatever his mission in life he should be taught the elements of canine courtesy. The pet hound, if he is to bring additional happiness to your home, must not be a nuisance to yourself, your guests or your neighbours, and the hound destined for work only, will learn his later lessons more easily if he has had some elementary training.

The essential good manners are:

1. To be well house trained.
2. To know his name and respond to it instantly.
3. To walk well with you on the leash.
4. To fully understand the word ' No '.
5. To sit on command.

These minimum requirements, once taught, will give the hound a firm basis with which to take his place in your life and act as a foundation for later training. They will build up your control, thus making any later problems that might arise easier to deal with. An experienced trainer is not needed to teach these lessons, in fact a keen child can do it, and in so doing will himself learn quite a lot.

I am strongly opposed to Bloodhounds going to training classes—such classes do an excellent job but not for Bloodhounds, and especially not if they are destined to be shown or hunted. Bloodhound temperament is such that to the fullest possible extent he must be asked, not told, to obey. The lessons should be started in the order given and each can overlap the next one or two.

HOUSE TRAINING

If you bought your puppy at six or eight weeks old start this training immediately. Provided you never let a ' mistake ' go unnoticed, young though he is, he will soon become clean in the house.

The most satisfactory method is, to begin with, place his bed or basket on several sheets of newspaper, having the paper surrounding the bed to the width of about one yard. You will find with most puppies that they prefer to relieve themselves just outside the bed and seldom soil their bedding.

If you catch your puppy making a puddle on the carpet or the floor, and not in the proper place, pick him up immediately and put him on the paper. When he behaves well, praise him and let him know you are pleased. He will soon learn that the newspaper and not the carpet is the proper place to ' spend pennies '.

As he gets used to the idea of using the paper, gradually move it each day, until you have the sheets in a position near the door. When he is accustomed to it in this position move it once again to a spot outside the door in the garden. You will find that it will only be necessary to have the paper outside the door for a couple of days as he will quickly learn that he has to go outside to relieve himself.

During this process you must, of course, take the pup outside in the garden after each meal, first thing in the morning, last thing at night and immediately after he wakes up from naps through the day. When he behaves like a gentleman tell him what a good boy he is and make a fuss of him.

It is, of course, a lot to expect of a young puppy that he should be clean in the house at night. However, once you have trained him to go outside during the day time, leave just one sheet of paper inside the door at night. When the time comes that the paper left overnight has not been soiled, then you can safely remove it and expect the pup to be clean. (It is worth mentioning here that there is now a proprietary preparation on the market, drops of which can be put on the newspaper. It is said that this will attract the puppy to its use.)

If, when he has been house trained, he occasionally makes a mistake indoors, do make sure that (a) he is perfectly fit and has no tummy upset, and (b) that he did not let you know beforehand that he wanted to go out. If he is fit and you are sure he didn't try to let you know, then smack him, put him outside and tell him, in no uncertain terms, that he is a naughty boy.

The system of ' rubbing their noses in it ' and putting down pepper is sometimes effective in the cure of persistently dirty animals. However, if you have trained your hound firmly and sensibly, these harsh and really outdated methods should be unnecessary.

We have dealt with house training but if a hound is to be kept in a kennel it is best to teach him to use his sleeping and living quarters as he would a home and not soil them. He should be taught to use the outside run of his abode to relieve himself. This is particularly necessary in the case of hounds inclined to soil their bedding—a modified form of house training will give the desired results.

TEACHING HIS NAME

The first essential in this lesson is to hold conversation with your hound. All dogs love to be spoken to but single words of command at this stage are not enough. When giving him his food ask him to come using his name, also use his name when making a fuss of him. He will soon learn that when called there is usually something good or exciting in store.

The use of a name in the early stages will greatly assist in his future training, and future lessons such as teaching him to come to you when off the lead will go

Plate V

Capt. and Mrs. C. H. Chapman with a 'Radnage' quartet, *c.* 1903.

Canis Dog Features.

Moore's drawing 1. "Margrave", *c.* 1905.

Canis Dog Features.

Brough's Chs. "Barnaby" and "Burgho", by L. Boellaars, 1894.

Canis Dog Features.

Plate VI

Ch. " Dark of Brighton ",
winner of 31 C.Cs.,
bred by the late Henry Hylden.

Photo by Avery's.

" Chatley Brilliar
mounted at the
Museum of
Natural H

*Courtesy of
Waterlow*

Black-and-Tan
American Coonhounds.

Courtesy of Leo C. Gilkey

smoothly, with the minimum of strain and irritation both to yourself and your hound.

LEAD TRAINING

Training to walk sensibly on a lead should be started when the hound is about three months old, unless he is intended to have a show career. If the show ring is the ultimate end the hound should be given complete freedom and no lead or road work until he is six or seven months old. It is unnecessary to trouble the pet puppy until he is three months old as obviously he will not be taken out into the streets until he has received the vital inoculations.

The first step is to buy a cheap collar, one that will fit comfortably now. From an economical point of view it would of course be better to buy a larger one which will fit the hound for some months to come, but collars purchased to fit the pup at different stages of his growth will make training easier. A collar too large is invariably too heavy and, unless it fits comfortably, the pup will only scratch and scrape at it until he gets it off. A harness should never be used (a) because, with Bloodhounds, these should be associated with tracking and (b) the continual use of these cause discomfort and restrict free movement of the legs and shoulders.

The pup should wear the collar for a short while, increasing the length of time daily, until he has it on in the morning and taken off when he goes to bed. You will find that, after the first couple of days, he will take no notice of the collar. Remember also, that this collar should bear your name and address and, if you have one, the telephone number.

E

Next, fix a small, light lead to the collar and let the pup run around dragging the lead. Do not attempt to hold him until he has overcome the first worry of having this peculiar thing fixed to him. When he is used to the lead pick it up and follow him, holding on to the lead but not attempting to alter the direction in which he wishes to run. Do this daily for about a week.

Now you can begin to try and control the hound on the lead. Be gentle but firm about it. Never tug violently or lose your temper when he pulls, otherwise you will put him into a nervous state and prolong the agony of training.

When he darts off, bent on some interesting smell, hold the lead firmly and call the hound, using his name. It will not take long for him to realize that when on the lead he must go your way without protest. It is unwise to let a child handle the puppy on a collar and lead until training is complete.

If, in spite of your training, the hound persistently pulls whilst on the lead, a choke collar should be used. It is unwise to use a chain choke on a Bloodhound but very effective leather ones can be purchased which will do the job just as well.

If you live in the country, or intend taking the hound to a locality where there is livestock you must, of course, make absolutely certain that he will be steady with other animals and birds. If at all possible the hound should be taken through cattle, sheep and poultry on a leash. If he shows no inclination to worry or chase them all well and good. If, however, he is unsteady this must be checked at once and with no half measures. The hound should be put on a choke collar and a long length of rope, taken back amongst the livestock and quietly walked around. If he does not respond to the word ' No ' when starting after them he must be jerked back really hard and made to understand that he must leave such things alone.

'No', and 'Sit'

The great importance of any dog understanding and obeying the word 'No' cannot be overstressed and in the case of a hound so powerful as that under review it is even more vital.

The way to teach obedience to the word is to use it and mean it whenever your charge does anything that is wrong. Misdemeanour can cover such things as stealing food, getting on to furniture, howling or barking, walking on flower beds, and so on.

If a hound on a leash misbehaves the word 'No' should be accompanied by a sharp pull on the leash and if this does not suffice a slap with a rolled newspaper should be given. When your hound attempts to take a piece of food that is not his it is no good restraining him and a few moments later giving it to him because he has soiled it as he may quickly learn to be artful.

Training a hound to sit on command is not difficult but takes time and patience. The easiest way is to take him out on his leash and every now and then stop and say 'Sit', pushing his hindquarters down whilst holding him steady with the leash. When he is sitting praise him and possibly give him a tit bit. At first he will probably only remain in a sitting position for a few seconds but with repetition he will learn that he must stay in that position until he is told he may move. When teaching him to stay in a sitting position whilst you walk away it must be remembered that he will obey more readily if he can see your face—it is therefore better if you *back* away from him until he has got the lesson firmly in his mind.

In general never start to give your hound a lesson if you yourself are tired or irritable, for the secrets of good dog training are patience, and perseverance, and never losing your temper during the handling. Bloodhounds do not need to be taught any lesson by the use of brute force and the whip. You will achieve far more by the use of a scolding voice and a slap than you will with a lash. Lastly, it is useless to mete out any punishment unless you are absolutely sure that the hound can really understand why he is being punished.

Newcomers to Bloodhounds, and those who keep a hound as a pet, find that a number of interesting additional activities apart from the act of hound ownership can be enjoyed.

The two breed clubs cater for all those who are interested in the breed, whether they own a hound or not, or whether they own one hound or fifty. Membership is well worth while and the clubs are always available to give help and advice . . . their function is to cater equally for everyone's interests and to further the good of the breed.

Anyone wishing to attend their first dog show need feel no qualms, they can be assured of a friendly courteous welcome, and numerous people will be willing to guide them. Fuller details of how to enter and show dogs are given in other volumes but details of shows are given in the dog trade papers and the secretaries of these shows will gladly supply information.

There are several classes of shows, the most junior being the match meetings, and we graduate from there to the sanction show, the limited show, the open show, and to the most important of them all, the championship show. At the smaller shows Bloodhounds have to compete with various other varieties or groups of dogs and hounds, but at the larger events special classes are provided for the breed.

Details of how to train your hound to hunt have been given, and those interested in such work have no doubt had great fun in so doing. If you need further guidance in hound training the breed clubs hold training days and, of course, the ultimate is to compete in the various stakes at the Field Trials.

CHAPTER V

CHOOSING THE SIRE

HAVING carefully analysed past records. I have come to the conclusion that, with Bloodhounds, the sire is more dominant in producing good quality stock than the dam, although this rule does not universally apply in other breeds. In this connection an early view of Mr. Everett Millais is of interest:

A pedigree animal is not merely an animal which has a pedigree, for as a pedigree it may be that of the greatest mongrel with the vastest extent of blue blood, but a pedigree animal is one who by his pedigree shows that he has been inbred enormously without any deterioration in quality; and the value of a pedigree animal, whether it be dog, pig, sheep, horse or bull, is in the fact that in comparison with a non-inbred animal it has the power of impressing on its progeny its own form and external characteristics, which no animal has to such an extent if it is not bred on these lines.

Why do people use pedigree bulls in preference to others? Why do people go for thoroughbreds, pedigree stud dogs—and so on?

It is because their stock is improved in the direction of the sire, not on that of the dam, and with these facts before us, which I might largely add to, we have standing proofs that the dictum that the

sire generally determines the form and external
characteristics is not open to modification except-
ing in the case of mongrels, where it is impossible
to form any opinion as to the results.

Some of our finest looking hounds have been produced from quite ordinary bitches, and certain sires,
though not in every case themselves outstanding in looks,
have had the ability to produce consistent quality with
the occasional flyer thrown in. The outstanding post-
war example of this is the Viscountess Waverley's
" Westsummerland Montgomery of Bre-Mar-Har-Ros ".
When choosing a mate for your bitch make the
selection carefully, and however great the distance, go to
the best available stud. Because of the difficulties we
shall now discuss, see that the dog you have chosen
regularly begets puppies and is keen on his job. It is a
great advantage if two or more stud dogs are available
at the kennel you visit as, if one will not mate, the other
may oblige.

Bloodhounds are notoriously difficult to get mated.
Many so-called stud dogs are completely disinterested in
the bitch, even when she is ready for mating and, while
some make rather feeble efforts to mate, they really have
not a clue. A great majority of bitches, even those who
have produced puppies before and are now quite ready
for mating, resist violently, but this is absolutely no
excuse for them to go away unmated as it is a well-known
trait in bitches of this breed.

BREEDING CONTRACTS

Here we digress for a moment to discuss two very important agreements which are often entered into. For

example where possible puppies are offered in lieu of cash payment, to avoid any subsequent misunderstanding it is essential, even when dealing with friends, that an agreement should be put into writing. In fact the most common contracts are in connection with bitches on breeding terms, and with stud fees.

In the first of these contracts the person accepting puppies is advancing credit and taking a gamble on there ever being any puppies, so he or she is entitled to a somewhat greater reward than on a cash transaction.

The usual contract of breeding terms is an arrangement where a bitch is loaned or disposed of for the considerations of which some or all of her future puppies go to the owner of the bitch at the time of the contract. On such an arrangement the whole matter is admirably covered by the Kennel Club Rules and Regulations, section ' D ' (' Regulations for the Loan or Use of a Bitch for Breeding Purposes '), and for a fee of £1 the transaction can be registered on a form provided by the Kennel Club.

Under section 3 of these regulations, it is essential to record who is to be responsible for choice of the stud dog and payment of the fees.

Covering stud service the fee is paid for the use of the dog, not for the resulting puppies. Reputable breeders will always offer a free service to the same bitch should she fail to conceive, subject to the dog still being in their possession, but it is always essential for the contracted terms to be clearly understood.

Very frequently a fee is not paid, the owner of the stud dog agreeing to take the pick or first choice of the litter. This arrangement must also be put in writing, although the custom is so widespread that in the event of legal argument it would most probably be admitted as ' custom of trade'. If there is only one puppy in the resulting litter this, strictly speaking, becomes the property of the stud dog owner. The puppy which is to be given in lieu of the fee cannot be registered by the breeder, but only by the new owner as the declaration on the Kennel Club registration form clearly states 'I/we certify the above particulars are true to the best of my/our knowledge and belief and the dogs I/we apply to register under Kennel Club Rules and Regulations are solely and unconditionally my/our property and have not been registered previously with the Kennel Club or any other recognized body'. I feel it would help if the Kennel Club drew up rules and an agreement form to cover stud services.

When a hound is offered at public stud he should be a proved sire of living puppies, be of a hundred percent sound temperament and free from viciousness or nerves, and he should be trained to be handled while mating his bitches, and to mate them however difficult they may be.

It is grossly unfair to potential customers who travel their bitches often over long distances, only to find the chosen stud is just not up to the work, either through lack of training or condition. If a hound is not proven or trained the facts should be stated and no fee charged until his first living puppies arrive into the world.

To get the best out of a stallion hound he should be strongly muscled and in really hard condition, probably some seven pounds below his best show weight. It is always difficult to combine show condition with stud condition as there is a foolish tendency for some specialist judges to prefer hounds to be exhibited somewhat overweight. The diet of a stud dog should be of the highest quality and he must be well exercised.

When a heavy hound mates a bitch the nails of his front feet tend to rake her so the front nails of a stud dog must be kept short with the ends rounded by filing. Should someone have neglected to remove the dew-claws these also should be kept short and rounded.

Fading puppies are discussed elsewhere but it would be a step forward to breeding healthier stock if stud dogs had throat swabs and blood samples taken and tested once yearly, when any irregularities in condition could be rectified.

MATING

The natural mating method of Bloodhounds—that is where dog and bitch are just turned loose in a paddock or stable, entails too much risk of failure and too much risk of damage to the dog or bitch. When two strange hounds are turned loose together in the hope of their mating there is a possibility of either serious fighting with possible damage to one or both hounds (if they are left alone one could be killed and, even if attended, anyone breaking up the fight could be bitten, for enraged hounds intent on each other can easily bite the humans they love in the heat of such a moment), or if they succeed in mating dog or bitch can damage each other by constant dragging about while ' tied '.

The correct thing to do to get a pair of Bloodhounds mated is to have three people present and to proceed as follows: check the bitch to ensure that there is no stricture to prevent the entry of the dog, and apply a little ' Vaseline ' (the sort that carries no odour) to the vagina.

The bitch must wear a well fitting leather collar and her mouth should be taped by tying an old stocking round the muzzle. This should be placed around the muzzle in the form of a ' U ', and the first knot tied on top of the muzzle, while the ends should then be brought down and tied again under the jaw. Now the two ends should be brought along each side of the head, looped through the top of the collar, and tied in a bow.

One person should now hold the bitch very firmly by the collar, one hand being each side of the neck. The stud dog should then be brought in and allowed to run around freely to smell the bitch and accustom himself to the people present. The stud dog should now be put on a long (five to six feet) leather leash and one person should keep hold of this and use it to lead or pull the dog away from the bitch when instructed. The dog should now be allowed to mount the bitch and the person holding her should remain firm. As the dog mounts the bitch the third person should move in to steady the bitch, stop her from sitting down, and if necessary, to assist the dog. If the dog is becoming so excited that he appears to be wasting his efforts, this third person should signal the one holding the lead to move him away for a few moments' relaxation.

The mating, having been effected with a ' tie ', and the dog turned back, the hounds should be held firm by two people. The tie usually lasts from ten to thirty minutes —and is the cue for the third person to go and make tea, by now so much needed by all.

The frequency with which a stud dog can be used is a matter of controversy. In the U.S.A. some sound research has been done by John H. Boucher, R. H. Foote and R. W. Kirk. Their study, reported in the *Cornell Veterinarian*, states: ' The quality of sperm remains high and the utilization of sperm at a maximum if a dog is used at stud every second day. Although he may be used oftener for a day or two, the sperm reserves are depleted after four or more ejaculations are obtained in

four days. Sperm obtained from fourteen daily collec-
tions and stored for twelve days at five degrees centigrade
lived for a satisfactory period, but not as long as sperm
collected less often '.

The demand for Bloodhound stud dogs is so small that
the foregoing shows there is no possibility of a hound
being over worked. As stallion hounds in this breed get
so little work it is best at present if they serve each bitch
that comes to them twice—subject of course to the owner
of the bitch agreeing.

To serve a bitch once seems to leave a dog hound un-
satisfied and restless, even noisy, for a couple of weeks
and he looses appetite and condition whereas if he mates
twice he seems to be quite happy. The matings should
of course be on successive or alternate days, not on the
same day.

Choosing the Dam

Not every one, even long established breeders, can
have Champion bitches to breed from, but well-bred
bitches correctly cared for and mated to top-class stallion
hounds can and do produce puppies as good as those
bitches who excel in looks, and who have an impressive
list of show bench wins. It is therefore possible to breed
successfully from any well-bred bitch.

The owner of the pet bitch frequently seeks advice
whether to breed from her. It can certainly be fun, is
instructive to any family, and is indeed good for the
bitch. However, unless there is a specially helpful family
quite a lot of extra work will fall to someone—most
probably the wife.

When breeding with a pet bitch the owner must never

forget the responsibilities to the breed in general; because the litter is 'just for the good of the bitch' it is still no good reason to breed from the nearest available dog. The aim should always be to produce the highest quality puppies possible.

With a large heavily boned breed such as this it is not advisable to breed until the second season, although if a bitch does not come into season for the first time until after one year of age no harm will be done if she is bred from. It is usual to miss a season between each litter but if the bitch has really regained condition and vigour and has not reared too large a litter no harm is done to breed from her on successive seasons, should some special reasons prevail for so doing. However, no bitch should be bred from every time unless she is irregular. If the bitch *is* irregular in her season it may be necessary to breed on each occasion.

On the whole Nature controls things very well and a bitch seldom conceives unless her condition warrants it. However, I cannot stress too strongly that however good the bitch she can only produce according to the quality of the stud dog used and the correctness of the food and vitamin supplements with which she is supplied.

Bloodhound bitches vary very much with regard to the time when they have the first heat, which can be at any time between eight and fourteen months of age. Should the bitch not have had a heat by the latter age, professional advice can be sought. The subsequent period between heats will vary between six and nine months, and in some cases, intervals of as much as one year will occur.

Your part of the job to assist the brood bitch to produce the best possible puppies must begin before, and well before, she is mated. She must be in excellent health, not overweight, and free from skin trouble, external and internal parasites. Even if an overweight bitch conceives, the surplus fat could exaggerate any possible whelping difficulties. If at all possible the internal parasites (worms) should be got rid of before mating, but under veterinary supervision a bitch can be wormed up to three weeks after mating. It is advisable to revaccinate the bitch against distemper so that the transfer of immunity to this disease from the dam to her whelps will be greater. It is also advisable to consult your veterinary surgeon to see what he advocates to guard against 'fading' of the puppies when they are born.

We have discussed the choice of stud dog but it is essential that the owner of the dog which you wish to serve your bitch is advised well in advance of the day and time when you wish to take your bitch for mating. With regard to the stud fee, this is paid for the stud service and not for the puppies likely to be produced. Most owners of stud dogs will provide a free service if the bitch fails to conceive, but in order to exclude the possibility of any argument of misunderstanding, the service conditions should be clearly written down and retained by both parties. The choice of the day on which to mate the bitch must be carefully chosen. The length of time a bitch is in season varies from two to four weeks (usually three), and the best time for mating seems to vary between the ninth and fourteenth day.

During the first three or four weeks of pregnancy do not force the bitch to lead an unnatural confined life. With food the emphasis must be on quality. By this I do not mean the most expensive foods, but protein rich foods, supplemented with vitamins and minerals. Normal exercise for the first four weeks should be allowed unless the weather is unduly hot. Robust play and jumping should be avoided and under no circumstances should a bitch be kenneled with other hounds after she is four weeks pregnant. For some reason pregnant bitches give off some smell which seems to incite members of the group of hounds who hunt by scent to fight. Even hound puppies will attack a heavily in-whelp bitch.

As pregnancy advances increase the quantity of food by increasing the number of meals—as for puppies, the secret is little and often. At the later stages of pregnancy raw liver is of especial value.

WHELPING

The bitch should be allowed to become accustomed to the place in which she is to whelp at least ten days before the puppies are due. The larger kennels have fitted whelping rooms but many places, such as a garage or garden shed, can be converted, provided they are dry, draught free and well ventilated. The whelping box or bed for a Bloodhound bitch should be at least three feet by four feet, with sides about six inches high.

With the unpredictable British weather an infra-red lamp should be available winter and summer. Except in extreme weather the height of the lamp (and for Bloodhounds I prefer the red or bright emitter) should be not less than three feet from the floor of the bed. As puppies gain strength the height of the lamp should be increased until (again unless the weather is extreme) the use of the lamp can be discontinued by the time the pups are three weeks old. An excellent account of the use of this type of heating apparatus appears in the illustrated section (pp. 52-55, and 87) of *The*

Papillon Handbook in this series, by Peggy and Bob Russell Roberts.

The best bedding for a bitch to whelp on is newspaper. This is warm and easily disposed of when soiled. When the pups are three days old the bedding should be changed to straw, and preferably wheat straw.

The bitch will become fidgety the day before the puppies arrive but if you are in any doubt her temperature can be taken. This will drop from the normal 102°F. to 99°F. or 100°F. about twelve hours before she is going to whelp. More often than not the bitch will refuse food the day before, but occasionally they will carry on eating up to the birth of the first puppy.

Most bitches prefer to have their litters alone, without help, but it is wise to look at her, taking care not to disturb her, from time to time to see that all is going well. If you find the bitch is biting the cords too close to the puppies stay and assist her, breaking them yourself. If the cords are bitten off too short there is danger of infection or hernia. Puppies usually arrive at intervals of ten to thirty minutes. If the time between puppies appears overlong, that is, an hour or more, your veterinary surgeon should be called, as a puppy may be presented in the wrong position and require expert assistance to enable the bitch to pass it.

It is unwise to try and prevent the bitch eating the placenta or afterbirth, as it is natural for her to do so and from it she derives a certain amount of nourishment and substances which encourage her to strain and pass the next puppy.

As each puppy is cleaned she will push it round in front of her and nudge it until it begins to feed. When another pup is born she will, of course, ignore those she already has. This will do them no harm; in fact a bit

Plate VII

The celebrated " Nick Carter ",
a Bloodhound responsible for over 600
American arrests and convictions.

Canis Dog Features.

dy Waverley's
k of
Vestsummerland "
with
" Coral "
and " Emily ".

Mr. and Mrs.
Oliphants'
Ch.
" Chatley Blazer ",
by Emms, 1905.

Canis Dog Features.

Plate VIII

Mr. H. S. Lloyd
with a brace of 4½ months puppies.

Photo by Sport & General.

English Bloodho
an American
Bloodhound
Bloodhound—
Otterhound cr
at the ' of Ware '
training ke

Photo by Daily Herald.

The Dumfriesshire Foxhounds, a pack of black-and-tan hounds.

of pushing around will help them to breathe properly. The only point to watch for is that one puppy does not get pushed behind the bitch and laid on. If this does happen, gently move the pup and place it among its brothers and sisters in front of the bitch.

If the process of whelping takes a long time, say all day, drinks of warm milk and glucose should be offered at intervals, taking care not to disturb the bitch in so doing. She may take a little milk but, should she be disinclined to drink, do not press her. It is best not to worry the bitch with food until she has quite finished whelping and has settled down with the pups. If she does not eat at all the day she has whelped it is nothing to worry about. However, if she refuses food the following day try and tempt her with pieces that you know she likes.

After whelping, each puppy should be examined every three or four hours for the first few days, and should any puppy be constantly crying or not full up with food your veterinary surgeon should be asked to look at it. You may just have a poor runt puppy but it may be some trouble which could affect others in the litter and early protection can save valuable stock.

While the bitch is suckling emphasis must be on plenty of high quality meals, with ample raw meat and milk. It is essential that the bitch should have a plentiful supply of clear, cool water and she should be given a choice of plain water or that to which a little anti-acid has been added. She will know which she needs and drink from the basin that suits her best.

The Young Puppy

The advice on whelping gave instructions on how to

F

check the puppies to make certain they have not been born with any infection carried from the dam.

When puppies are examined you should also see that none have been born with cleft palates and should any have this they should be painlessly put to death. You should also watch for any infection of the navel which may have been caused by the bitch biting off the cord too close to the body. Some bitches are a little rough with their puppies and cause ruptured navels. If the rupture is small it is nothing to worry about as it will not be apparent when the hound grows to maturity, if however, there is a large rupture this can be operated on by a veterinary surgeon when the puppy is about seven weeks old.

If you want to rear good quality puppies and no foster mother is available, the maximum number you allow the bitch is nine. If the litter is much larger than this there are usually some weaklings, or some who will have bad faults according to the breed Standard, and these are the ones which should be disposed of. If you are unable to make a decision consult an experienced Bloodhound breeder. If no one with specific experience is available any really practical dog breeder can probably give useful help. The culling must be done early for if there are too many puppies one of the best may suffer as a result of overcrowding.

If you have a range of different coloured puppies keep some of each colour but not too many liver-and-tans as these, though the least common colour, are hardest to sell.

At four days of age the dew-claws should be removed. And bent sterns too can be treated then: if the kink is near the tip, remove the bent part, but if near the root leave alone and sell the pup as a pet. Gums should be examined to ensure they are nice and pink, for if they appear grey or whitish the pups may be anæmic and professional advice should be sought.

At about ten days the eyes will begin to open and careful watch should be kept to see that they open cleanly and to their full extent. If after opening the eyelids tend to stick or are a little mucky they should be gently bathed with warm water. The subject of inversion is discussed elsewhere but if it is apparent in any puppy the necessary operation should be carried out as early as possible lest ulcers on the eye or other damage is caused. Any affected puppy must certainly be dealt with before sale and the new owner advised accordingly.

As the puppies begin to cut their teeth a most careful watch must be kept as occasionally the large upper teeth will dig into the lower lip and cause holes which, if infected, cause ulcers which are most difficult to cure. The mouth must also be checked before the sale of a puppy to ensure that it is neither undershot nor overshot. Either of these malformations will spoil a puppy for show purposes but will be no detriment to a pet hound or for tracking. Such a puppy should not be purchased if one wants to breed, as bad mouths are hereditary and such stock should not be bred from.

It is to be sincerely hoped that your Bloodhound will be with you for many years, and bring something of extra value into your life. Selection therefore should not be rushed.

If your pup is required to grow into a pet or **Companion dog** choose the one whose personality appeals to you most. A wise precaution if paying a high price for a puppy is to buy it subject to a veterinary surgeon's certificate of health being given. This will cost about one guinea and the fee should be paid by the purchaser. Such an examination protects both buyer and vendor. Should it be decided to dispense with the foregoing, check the following points:

Eyes—these should be bright and free from any matter or watery discharge. The haw should be nice and red, and there should be no inversion.

Mouth—the gums should be really pink; whitish or grey gums are a sign of ill-health. The tongue should be clean and the breath sweet with almost a faint smell of chocolate.

Skin—examine the skin to see that it is clean and free from external parasites. Especially check the top of the head and ears, and if the hair is at all sparse here scratch or scrape the inside of the ear with your finger nail. If the hound shows a reaction by twitching a hind leg suspect mange and make further enquiries.

Nerves—stamp on the floor or clap your hands hard. Probably most of the litter will scamper away but those with sound nerves will stop and look enquiringly. Those who stay away and continue to cower should be viewed with suspicion.

The show puppy should have none of the faults for which the puppy should next be examined but they do not detract from its companion qualities. The presence of such faults reduce the value of a puppy nevertheless.

Mouth—this should show a scissors bite, with the lower front teeth just inside the upper.

White markings—these are permissible on the chest or feet but not on the legs, on top of the muzzle, between the eyes or on the skull.

Stern—this should be completely straight, terminate in a natural point and have no fixed kink or bend.

Navel—this should protrude but little, if at all, but a lump the size of the tip of the thumb is no disadvantage. One larger should be suspect.

Bone—this should be straight and thick in the legs, with the ribs sound and well formed. There should be no sign of rickets.

To choose a **Show prospect** the examination should now become more thorough and attention paid to detail. Compare puppy with puppy and pick the one excelling in these points:

Head—the head should show room to grow to an adequate length without coarseness of skull and to have ample depth and squareness of lip and, even at six weeks of age, abundant wrinkle.

Eyes—these should give promise of being dark when they reach their final colour.

Ears—these should be of ample length, not thick to the touch and be set on below the level of a line taken back from the eye.

Neck—should have some length.

Shoulders—should be checked for correct placement.

Outline—set the puppy up as you would a mature dog and see that the front is straight and true, the body with depth of brisket and spring of rib, the topline level and the quarters parallel with a good bend of stifle.

Stern—this should be checked when the hound is playing and if it is too gay, that is curled to the back, it is doubtful if it will ever settle. If either parent has the fault it is even more doubtful.

Feet—these should be strong, well knuckled and with depth.

Overall—select for immense strength and exaggeration of show points.

The **working hound** has to be selected for his unseen qualities. In my book *The Beagle Handbook,* published in this series, I wrote: ' The hidden qualities are nose, voice, stamina and drive, although, without conformity with the breed Standard, the first three are not likely to be of the best.'

The breed Standard is, of course, drawn up to describe the physical form of a hound able to fulfil his mission in life. At this stage of the breed's development hounds of most bloodlines will hunt, but I fear if some kennels continue to search for looks and disregard working ability this state of affairs will not linger on. A pet hound of any strain can therefore give a lot of fun while hunting and will do the job reasonably well, but if the aim is to work a hound really seriously and to win at Trials careful choice must be made.

To make a personal selection for serious work I would analyse Field Trial results and buy something sired by, or out of, the older generation whose stock has been well and truly proved by results. But even in this choice I would go for a hundred percent Bloodhound and avoid any Foxhound outcross. This is only my whim, however, because when hunting for pleasure I prefer to win with pure blood, having some pretensions to size and looks, than with an undersized or ugly beast.

FEEDING

Feeding a hound is not the complex difficult matter that many would have us believe but if a hound is to be easy to feed and a good doer later on some early trouble and effort on the part of the person preparing and offering the food will prove well worth while. The two main factors of good feeding are first to present the food attractively and palatably and of such a size that the hound can comfortably eat it without suffering inconvenience from his large lip and loose skin around the mouth. It is extremely difficult for a hound of this breed to eat squashed, mashed-up, soggy messes however much goodness is contained therein.

I am a great believer in a mincing machine for use in large kennels but minced food is no good for Blood-hounds. At the initial weaning stage the meat or offal should be scraped and at six weeks half-inch squares are probably the appropriate size, increasing to about two-inch squares for the adult hound.

It is absolutely essential that from the earliest age puppies should be got used to a very wide variety of tastes. If you start feeding your hound on Mr. Brown's biscuit and do so without variation for a year do not be surprised if all other makes are refused should this par-ticular brand fail to be available. If you must always use the same brands of biscuit do vary its flavour by soaking it with broths of different ingredients. The normal household condiments, herbs and vegetables not forgetting onion and leek can all be used intelligently to produce a variety of flavours.

Offal and meat are the natural foods and, if freely available at reasonable prices, are preferable to proprie-tary foods or cereals. Offal is purposely put before meat as I personally consider it of at least equal importance to muscle meat. When hounds kill game before getting to work on the muscle meat they always eat absolutely all of the insides (I refer, of course, to the kills of Fox-hounds, Harriers and Beagles). When sufficient flesh is not available use good quality dog biscuits preferably those made from whole wheat and some containing bone meal. It is an old-fashioned practice to feed hounds a pudding made of oatmeal and while appreciating that I strike at a solidly established practice I feel that this product is bad for hounds, at the very least it is an extremely uninteresting food for any dog. If there is some sound reason for not using a good quality hound meal I prefer flaked maize (watching always for skin irritation which it sometimes produces) and even potatoes cooked and fed with the skins left on.

When making your selection from the available biscuits and hound meals do choose varieties that do not crumble but retain their form after soaking and when mixing flesh with it try to keep the whole meal so that its pieces can easily be picked off the feeding dish.

The adult in normal health requires only one meal a day, this should be planned to fit in with your household routine and be timed so that the hound can go out for short exercise immediately after this. Leaving aside the finer points of condition required when preparing for the show ring give a quantity sufficient to give a good feel over the ribs. The weight is about right when you can feel the bones of the rib cage without much pressure and when the bones are not immediately noticeable to a light touch. Do not trust your eye but always lay on hands for a hound with a very good spring of rib can look fat when he is in fact pretty lean underneath.

Let us at this stage briefly discuss show condition. At a recent London championship show a judge commented that the Bloodhound ring, especially in the bitch classes, resembled a fat stock show. This comment was possibly justified; a hound should never be shown so fat that he could not, if suddenly called out of the show ring, go and hunt at a good pace over hard country.

Correct show condition is when the hound's coat is in

Plate IX

Mr. and Mrs.
R. Furness'
W.T. Ch.
" Raycroft Sailer ",
after the painting by
Evelyn Barnsley.

Mrs. M. Sadleir's
Ch.
" Dorset of
Barchester ".

Mrs. Y. Oldman
with Ch.
" Barsheen Jewel ".

Photo by Cooke.

Plate X

(*right*)

Head study of " Cromwell " (after a painting by Maud Earl).

(*below*)

Ch. " Dominator of Brighton ", owned by Mr. Hylden.

Photo by Fall.

(*below*)

Mr. Douglas Appleton exercising a brace of Champions.

Photo by Harley.

Plate XI

(left)

> The author's Ch. " Appeline Hector of West-summerland ".

(below)

> Ch. " Scarcity of Kelperland ",
> owned by Mr. Townson.

Photo by Pilgrim.

elow)

Mr. Douglas Henderson,
of Brisbane,
ith Chs. " Pluto " and
Wuthering Dulciana of
Dobrudden ".

Plate XII

(right)

The author's Int. Ch.
" Spotter of Littlebrook ",
winner 41 times out of 42 in the U.S.A.
and never beaten by a dog in Britain.

(below)

Mr. and Mrs. A. Langdale's
D. Ch. " Easebourne Tarquin ",
the only post-war Dual Champion.

Photo by Cooke.

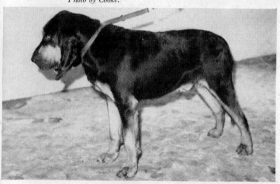

Mrs. Oldfield and
                Mr. Nichols'
                Ch.
" Dasher of Brighton ",
the only Bloodhound to
go BiS at a post-war
championship show.

Photo by Cooke.

full bloom and he is physically and constitutionally ready to go hunting, with the body nicely covered in flesh but showing some waist at the loins. Hunting condition, however, must never be confused with poor condition, for a hound in the latter state may be able to hunt for short distances but will lack stamina.

When feeding puppies it must be appreciated that no breed makes a more rapid daily weight gain and it is in the first six months of a hound's life that his permanent bone and body structure is built. In fact a moderate puppy very well reared will quite often finish up better than a brother who shows immense early promise but is not quite so well reared. Water makes up about half of a dog's live weight and is an indispensable element of all their tissues and secretions. Water is the cheapest part of dog flesh—there is no excuse, therefore, in not having it always available for puppies and adults. The only time water should be withheld is on veterinary advice during illness and when a dog is extremely tired and hot. On this latter occasion water should gradually be made available in small quantities.

I am not here going to set out a feeding chart for puppies. Bloodhound whelps can and do do well on the normal puppy routine which is known to most pet owners but if you require to build your hound into something a little bit better than its fellows three milk and five solid meals are a daily requirement from six weeks of age. The number of meals can be gradually decreased and the quantity of each meal increased until the adult is having a single meal daily.

When rearing your puppy act as I have already suggested and use a wide variety of foods: offals such as liver, tripe, heart and paunch; meat of all types including one-third fat, and do not despise the humble breast of mutton; fish of the cheaper varieties including herring which is excellent and if well boiled can be used in its entirety; small quantities of all vegetables after they have been well cooked, preferably with the addition of salt (but do not overdo it), and using the water to make broth.

The brood bitch and the stud dog need a diet of slightly higher quantity and quality than the domestic pet and the additional food should be of high protein value.

Vitamins play a very important part in the growth and health of the dog and should be given as additions to the diet of young stock, brood bitches and stud dogs. The two following vitamins are the ones which I consider most important for the Bloodhound.

VITAMIN B12. This I consider essential for the bitch during pregnancy and to puppies of six weeks old, and subsequently until growth is complete. Veterinary Cytamen 250 can be given by injection or Cytacon tablets can be given orally. The former is the most satis-factory method of dosing and as the use of the hypo-dermic syringe is so simple all breeders should learn how to use it. The vitamin helps appetite, growth and nerves.

VITAMIN D. This again I consider essential for satis-factory Bloodhound rearing or breeding. Without it the brood bitch may develop eclampsia or produce poor boned rickety puppies and the whelps without it never make sufficient bone or substance to become top-class show dogs. Massive dosage is recommended and again it can be given orally or by injection. It has been said that the presence of round worms reduces the efficacy of the vitamin if it is given orally and for this reason some people prefer injection, but personally I have always got the best results from a daily dose of 50,000 i.u.

CHAPTER VI

BREED PROBLEMS AND CARE

SEVERAL problems afflict the breed. There is no doubt that they are serious—in fact serious enough to warrant a special chapter, but not so widespread as to deter any prospective owner, provided he is careful in the selection of his stock. However, these difficulties must be squarely faced, fought and eliminated.

The most serious evil is bloat or distention which also occurs in other large breeds such as Borzois and Irish Wolfhounds. During the last few years this attacked many notable hounds, including Mrs. Y. Oldman's Ch. "Dazzle of Reynalton", Mr. and Miss Hylden's Ch. "Buccaneer of Brighton", and the importation from the U.S.A., Int. Ch. "Spotter of Littlebrook". With such a shortage of top-class hounds we can ill afford such grievous losses.

When visiting kennels in the U.S.A., I was confronted with the theory that a certain English strain was the cause of bloat—this theory, like so many others on the subject, was immediately discounted when I pointed out that "Spotter", who contained none of this particular blood, had 'blown up' and died from heart failure following the operation.

My own theory is that distention is most likely to occur in a hound overweight and a bit short of exercise. The sort of time this is likely to occur is when that extra bit of condition is required for show and exercise is reduced and food increased.

Mr. R. S. Townson, M.R.C.V.S. of Berkshire, has written a special section on distention for publication in this handbook. Mr. Townson, who specializes in small animal practice and is on the executive council of the British Small Animal Veterinary Association, is president of the Southern Counties B.S.A.V.A., and is also on the council of the British Veterinary Association, as well as being chairman of the Bloodhound Club and a successful breeder and exhibitor.

The important thing is to get any hound suspected to be suffering from bloat to the operating table with an absolute minimum of delay.

DISTENTION

(By R. S. Townson, M.R.C.V.S.)

Bloat, or acute gastric tympany, is a condition of certain breeds that has come to be regarded as a certain killer.

Bloodhounds, Deerhounds, Great Danes and Irish Wolfhounds especially appear most susceptible. The exact cause still remains unsolved. It appears that the condition is hereditary and a follow up of afflicted dog's pedigrees would appear to confirm that fact.

I am not at all convinced that meat-fed dogs are more prone than dogs fed on a meat-free diet. However, Whitney of Connecticut, U.S.A., states that he has bred bloat-free hounds, fed on a meat deficient diet. We cannot take his findings as conclusive because there is nothing to suggest that his hounds would or would not have developed bloat, with or without meat.

Even extensive trials with meat and non-meat-fed hounds, with controls, would not be conclusive unless carried out over a period of many years.

We do, however, know what happens, even if no theory proves the cause:

1. There is stenosis of the pylorus—a total stenosis.
2. This causes food to ferment in the strongly acid stomach enzymes and contents.
3. Gases are thus produced which rapidly distend the stomach.
4. Before the stomach is fully distended, there is torsion of this organ.
5. As a result of this twist it is now quite impossible to liberate these gases, with either emetics or parasympathetic stimulants. Indeed, the latter are strongly contra-indicated because of the accompanying acute heart depression.
6. With stomach distended, the vagus nerve is stimulated, causing a reflex depression of the heart.
7. Death from acute heart failure follows within a few hours of the initial symptoms.

How can we deal with this disease? Obviously we should find the exact cause of the pyloric stenosis, for until this is thoroughly investigated by veterinary surgeons engaged in active research on the subject there is little we can do, except treat the symptoms as they arise.

There is no doubt that if the condition can be

detected before the stomach twists, then an emetic (preferably apormorphine hydrochloride) will have the required effect. Vomiting will empty the stomach and at the same time will ease the spasm of the pylorus.

Unfortunately, the speed with which the stomach 'blows' is usually too rapid and efforts are usually too late. By this time the stomach has twisted and has also lost the power of vomiting.

Paracentesis into the stomach with a wide bore hypodermic needle may liberate a little of the gases, but immediate operation is necessary, preceded by injection of Coramine or caffein, or other heart stimulants.

Lapterotomy is performed, the stomach opened and the gases released. At once there is a perceptible improvement in the condition of the heart. As soon as the gases are released the stomach untwists back to normal.

This operation in itself is simple and straightforward. Unfortunately there is such acute depression of the heart that death often occurs within hours of the operation. Thus, speed is essential.

A study of recovered cases has revealed that the majority relapse later on. It would therefore appear that some form of prevention must be undertaken.

The first method is simple and the pylorus is resected down to the mucos, that is the muscle and outer serous coat of the pylorus is divided surgically, thus preventing further pyloric spasm.

The other method is a little more complicated and is called a gastro-enterostomy. This means that an opening is made in the stomach and another in the

duodenum, these two apertures are then joined together, enabling the gastric contents to pass directly
into the intestines, by-passing the pylorus.

It is a pity that funds are not available at this
time for research into this subject. One feels that
if the clubs for the breeds of dogs which are subject
to this condition could get together some headway
might be made. If these breed clubs would donate
sums of money to research on the matter, then perhaps we shall see some light on this, our most
dreaded complaint.

INVERTED EYELIDS

The next problem is concerned with inverted eyelids,
technically called entropion, which also occurs in a number of other breeds. Here the cause is definitely heredi-
ary. To some degree it is brought about by the type
of eye specified in the breed Standard and worsened
when breeders ignore the hereditary tendencies of the
condition.

The fault can be diagnosed by examining the eyes
when it will be seen that the eyelashes grow in such a
way as to come into contact with the actual eye, causing
initially a discharge, and if left untreated, ulceration of
the eye and damage to the sight. Cure is effected by
surgical methods. The operation should be carried out
immediately the condition is noticed and no puppy
suffering from this fault should be sold until it is rectified.

We all know the misery humans suffer when a single
eyelash gets into the eye, even though it is only there
for a few moments. Imagine, therefore, the misery and

anguish suffered by a hound allowed to go through life continually tortured by this fault solely because the owner does not get professional treatment.

In his excellent volume on training Bloodhounds the eminent American authority, Leon F. Whitney, D.V.M., states:

> I have spent many hours sitting beside strings of my dogs at shows, and have listened to the remarks of the crowd. At the Madison Square Garden show I kept records for two evenings and the majority of the people looking at the *good* ones— good by the show Standard—would glance at their red haws under the eyes and exclaim ' disgusting ', or ' what weird looking creatures '. Then I would hear someone say, ' Oh! here's a lovely one '. I would watch to see the ' lovely one ' and find it was the dog with the most satiny coat and the tightest eyes, showing the least haw. I like the extreme appearance—all Bloodhound breeders do—but let's be honest and admit the public doesn't. If I had my way, I would revise the Standard to say we want as little haw showing as possible. This has been done with other breeds—some Spaniels —to their great benefit.

I too feel this is correct, and if the suggestion were adopted, breeders would gain by having a more saleable product and would be able to stamp out this hereditary failing.

An example of the bolder eye is shown in the picture of Kent McClelland's Am. Ch. "Appeline Hemlock" This hound has won the highest honours in the U.S.A and before leaving England won, as a youngster before fully matured, the Cruft's Ledburn Trophy, and wa three times runner-up to the C.C. winners. This shows that the 'improved' eye does not prevent a successful show career.

A hereditary skin trouble exists in one particular strain. It is loosely described and treated as a form of mange and only those closely connected with the breed, or who have previously met the trouble give a correct diagnosis. So far the trouble is unnamed; it is not contagious and only occurs after the skin is broken. With a working breed it is impossible to prevent skin abrasions and when a hound carries a tendency to this form of skin trouble such abrasions do not heal. An area of skin larger than the actual wound becomes sore and infected, loses the hair and does not regain an even skin texture owing to the failure of complete healing. The muzzle is the most likely place for the trouble to occur but it can be widespread. Even when the affected area appears to be almost healed it erupts again and all attempts to make the hair return end in disappointment.

In any hound of this strain efforts should be made to avoid getting any broken skin, but should injury occur prompt dressing with a suitable germicide and scrupulous cleanliness may restrict the spread of the infection. Any scabs should be removed each day. Fortunately this occurs only in a bloodline which is not carried in many hounds.

TEMPERAMENT

Temperament is very very rarely bad in a puppy, but puppies of some particular bloodlines will develop nervousness or viciousness if subjected to incorrect treatment and handling. It must be appreciated that

G

shyness and a tendency to bite indiscriminately both stem from a hound's feeling of insecurity.

Always ask a Bloodhound for obedience, never tell him. Build up his confidence in yourself and the outside world, accustom him to surprise noises while he is young and show him that they do not hurt him. Never punish unless it is certain that the hound knows what he has done wrong. Punishment by tone of voice is always better than physical correction and if you must employ the latter a smack with a newspaper is all that is needed; never use the whip, and never punish a hound when your own temper is high.

Some breeders have said that temperament varies with colour but it has been stated that each colour in turn is wrong so the theory is proven nonsense!

Given correct handling from six weeks of age any hound can have a good temperament, but given wrong handling he can become as shy as a field mouse or vicious and uncertain.

We must now consider what to do with a hound with a damaged temper. Each case can only be treated on its merits. I have had hounds from pet homes and have found it impossible to train them in the essentials of good manners, while another, abandoned by professionals as incurably vicious, became—when asked and not told— completely lovable and never took another bite in anger.

With a nervous or shy animal modern tranquillisers, used only on veterinary advice, can help and cures are often effected. It is of course forbidden to use such tranquillisers to improve a hound's performance in Field Trial competition or in the show ring, and heavy and just would be the penalty on anyone proved to have used them for this purpose.

The hound of uncertain temper who takes a bite at or

attacks a person when he should not is indeed a difficult problem. Improvement can sometimes be effected, but complete certainty of good temper is rarely regained. It is foolhardy for an inexperienced person to take on such a hound who should be left to someone with ample time and experience.

EXTERNAL CARE

Bloodhounds, if not kept absolutely clean, tend to give off an odour which, in common with some other hounds, is even stronger than that of other breeds of dogs when cleanliness is neglected. The procedure that follows is not all essential but is planned for the owner who wishes the hound to attain an outstanding appearance.

A good hard brushing with, and not against, the hair for about ten minutes each day does as much good as an extra walk. Grooming should start from about eight weeks of age and if this is done the hound will grow to enjoy it and will co-operate with you as he gets older and will not fidget while he is being worked on. To commence, use a softish brush but by about six months of age a really stiff bristle brush should be in use.

If two brushes are kept and used week about with a good wash in between they will wear better and the bristles will keep stiffer. The best brush is one which your hand can grip comfortably but firmly and the bristles should be reasonably widely spaced so that the dirt does not clog at the base. A natural bristle is still to be preferred to the artificial substitutes. There is no need at all for the use of the comb; in fact, with the abundance of loose skin, it is quite easy to dig a tooth into the hound and make a sore spot.

If you wish to make the coat ' cherry ripe ' finish off after brushing with a clean dry washleather or velvet square, and once or twice weekly apply sparingly a good quality slightly oily coat dressing, or even a human hair cream. It must be remembered, however, that every trace of dressing must be removed before a hound is taken into the show ring.

After brushing a good massage with the palms of the hands over the back, flanks, loins and quarters gives additional lustre to the coat and helps conditioning. Where you wish to develop the muscles these should be rubbed up and down and across, the ruffled hair being afterwards smoothed down.

During grooming the ears should be checked inside and out. Inside to ensure there is no surplus wax or ear trouble developing, and outside to see there is no stale food attached to the hair where the ear has dangled in the food dish. If this has occurred wash in luke-warm water, and should any loss of hair occur, apply a dressing such as Viacutan.

Finally, after grooming, gently bathe the eyes with a luke-warm solution of boracic, proprietary eye lotion or cold weak tea.

Once weekly, during grooming, the teeth should be checked. If they are really clean do not touch them at all. If decomposed food is caught between the teeth clean this out with an ordinary toothbrush and if a hard deposit is there then scale them. While teeth scaling is not difficult after practice the beginner would be well advised to study pages 253-4 of Clifford Hubbard's *The Complete Dog Breeders' Manual* (Sampson Low, Ltd.), 1954. Once weekly also (this should in fact have happened since birth) see the toenails are short and cut them if necessary.

If this routine is carried out regularly it takes surprisingly little time and the time it does take will be amply rewarded by the improved appearance and well being of your hound. Even during illness this procedure in a milder form is best continued, for a sick hound becomes a sicker one if he is left dirty.

I cannot stress too strongly how much easier the foregoing is to carry out if it is started directly you get your hound, and any restiveness should be firmly dealt with from the outset.

A good bathing every three months will be beneficial, but should not be performed within a week of a show or some of the natural bloom will be missing from the coat. Luke-warm water should be used, together with a high quality dog shampoo. After washing the coat should be rinsed at least twice, and if a small quantity of vinegar is used in the first of the rinsing waters it does help to get the soap out.

If this procedure is followed regularly no extra coat preparation is necessary, except for a final polish, before a hound goes into the show ring, but if a hound has been neglected the foregoing should be carried out in an intensified form.

Some exhibitors run hounds over with an oily rag before they go into the ring but this should not be needed unless grooming has previously been neglected. It is in any case likely to be offensive to the judge who has to handle the animal, and anyway it is an offence to leave dressing on or in the coat.

The amount of exercise a hound needs is quite a controversial matter, and does vary considerably from hound to hound. Certainly, until at least six months of age, no forced exercise should be given, the hound being allowed to take what he wants about the house and garden or in his kennel and run.

I find that about three miles a day, on hard ground or roads, in one or two sessions, plus some ten or fifteen minutes' free galloping is all that is needed to keep a hound really fit. Hounds kept as house pets, and who are correctly fed, can and do get by very satisfactorily on less as they tend to get quite a lot of exercise pottering about the home.

Hounds from some particular bloodlines, however, are extremely hard to get muscle on the hindquarters and these need more work if they are to move well behind. In this respect some strong galloping uphill is very beneficial.

When a hound has paper feet or spreading toes many people give any amount of additional exercise to improve the feet. Good feet however are bred not made, and while the extra exercise will no doubt benefit you it will help the hound's feet but little.

Some of a hound's exercise must be for his pleasure; he must be allowed to sniff and meander as he will, but the part that is given to condition him must be carried out at a sharp, well maintained pace so that all muscles are brought into play. If a hound is being kept for work as a man trailer he needs more exercise and to be kept in harder condition. This I find applies not only to Bloodhounds but to all hounds primarily bred for field work, as I made clear in my *The Beagle Handbook* (Nicholson & Watson), 1959. Incidentally, as I have well over-run my allotted space in the present volume I would refer readers to my Beagle book for a section on general health, where in pages 110-132 the principal illnesses are fully discussed.

CHAPTER VII

TRAINING AND TRIALS

MANY people decide to have a Bloodhound because they like the breed, but the interest of training it to hunt man and possibly enter at Field Trials is a fascinating extra to hound ownership.

A pet hound of any strain can give a lot of fun while hunting and will do the job reasonably well, but if the aim is to work a hound really seriously and to win at Trials choice must be made with a view to this end.

The theories and methods of hound training are many. The one I am going to advance now has two distinct advantages—(*a*) The hound is, when finally trained, likely to remain always completely under control of the handler, and (*b*) When a companion hound is to be trained to track for the pleasure of the hunting he gives, the owner can start training directly he gets a puppy and while early enthusiasm prevails.

The ultimate aim may be to hunt man for the fun of it, or to compete at Field Trials, or even for an official job of work. Training is the same and cannot begin too soon, providing the puppy is not allowed to get bored or overtired and is treating the matter as a game.

TRAINING TO HUNT

Training should be in the following three stages, each stage to blend with the succeeding one:

1. To teach the young puppy that he has a nose and that to use it is amusing, pleasant and rewarding.

2. To gradually convert puppy playtime and the in-discriminate use of the nose towards the ultimate aim of hunting man and to obtain steady control.
3. To have the hound hunting man, and only man, under complete control of the huntsman.

It is quite easy to teach the puppy from about seven weeks onwards that he has a nose and will be rewarded when he uses it. The reward to consist of a favourite titbit and an affectionate petting, or of a meal.

Let this then be a game you and the puppy play a few times weekly. With one of the daily meals get someone to hold the puppy while you let it sniff and taste, then drag the food dish away a few yards and tuck it behind a box or shrub—that is, somewhere out of sight. When this is done let both people utterly ignore the pup until he has found and eaten the food. Do not worry at this stage if the pup sees where you hide the food but keep varying the hiding place, and gradually increase the distance it is taken away.

When, after a week or two, this game with a purpose is going well, start dragging the food away with the puppy held so he does not see where it goes, then let him be turned loose to find it. As this lesson progresses and the hound gains confidence, begin to use the words or cries you have planned for use in your ultimate hunting. Increase the distance and the time lag before releasing the pup, but if any sign of lack of interest is shown by the hound give up for that day. If, on any occasion, the puppy fails to find the food he must be very quietly led or eased towards it.

The lessons will also have to be missed if the appetite is poor for any reason and food not keenly wanted. As the hound's interest and confidence increases get some off-scene distractions going—such as the rattling of tin cans or the radio played loudly nearby. Should a second pair of hands not be available, put a wire door on a large tea chest or suitable box and shut the hound in while he sniffs food through the wire, then release him to seek.

The other game, which must never be started until the hound has worked off some steam and got used to the distractions of the place, can be given in the garden or in a field. Pet and play with your pup for a few moments, run a few feet and let him catch up with you. Then pet and play again—gradually working the distance up so you can duck behind a tree of bush, momentarily out of sight. The pup will probably come but, if not, call him up. If he still won't come just resume your walk and try again next day. If he comes pet him and give him a favourite titbit.

Even at this stage attempts to run off to some diversion justify a gentle rating. Here again, as progress is made, bring into play your hunting cries in such a manner that the hound's movements or actions coincide with what instructions you will ultimately want to convey. Likewise, if you intend to use a hunting horn (and please do) in your work, now is the time to let the hound get used to it. Once the hound is seeking you get a second person to play with him and disappear while you stand by to give help and encouragement as the situation demands. The hound will eventually have to do his job on the harness and it is at this stage of the training that is the appropriate time to let the hound become used to wearing it. However, once he is used to the feel of it only put it on for training sessions (harness design is discussed on page 101). When this variation has satisfactorily progressed, couple a light line to the harness and slowly and subtly establish a little control.

I must again stress the need to avoid all possibility of boredom with a hound so young. As you are going along numerous ideas for variations of the lesson will occur to you—so try them. If you want the hound to use his voice as he works it is during these lessons that foundations can be laid, for in the early stages of chasing your hound will almost certainly make some whimpering cries, and these should according to your wishes be encouraged or discouraged.

This early work will carry on until the hound is about six or seven months of age. Though not essential it helps if at this stage you or a friend have an old steady hound who will track (a Basset who will hunt the clean boot is ideal). Let your pup get a sight of him at work and should he try to join in then encourage him.

Between now and the age of nine months, the serious facts of life, and that playtime ends and enjoyable work time begins, must be instilled into the hound. Gradually the clean boot, and only that, must be hunted and from now on the hound should never be allowed to hunt the handler. He must now be taught to be completely steady on livestock and game. If he shows signs of riot it must be checked immediately by taking him back amongst the poultry, sheep or cattle on a very long rope and a chain choke collar. When he attempts to chase pull him back really hard and chastise thoroughly.

Until growth is complete, make a temporary butterfly type harness from soft webbing, to tie or buckle under the chest. Before asking the hound to play your game with a purpose, fit his harness on somewhat ostentatiously so that he senses your actions have a meaning, then start the lesson at once. It will of course have been necessary to get the hound used to wearing the harness in kennels before this stage, but never exercise on the harness. It must mean one thing, and one thing only—'off to work we go'. If you are using the horn, give an appropriate signal once the harness is on, to alert the hound.

Instruction on the correct method of identification should begin at six months and the person sought should kneel so that, when found, the hound's feet can be lifted to his chest or shoulders, and a little later on the reward for the find should only be given when the hound is in this position.

The detail given for this early instruction should not imply that it is not possible to train an older hound. Hounds of over five years, without previous working experience or training have been taught to put up very creditable performances. When taking on an older hound it is necessary to assess his aptitude and adapt methods to suit him.

The final stage of training should develop from the second stage, with the hound hunting only the clean boot, both completely free, and on a line.

Every experienced hunting person has his own methods and pet theories and the foregoing is devised for those who have a pup and are anxious to get started. The early work may not make your hound any better than one whose training does not commence until he is a couple of years old but you will both have had some fun and your hound will be surely under control. The critics of the foregoing method may say it relies too much on natural aptitude. Well, if the Bloodhound hasn't natural aptitude breeders over the last century have been doing a pretty poor job!

The 'White Isle' kennels of the U.S.A. have carried out experiments by dividing litters of puppies, training one half while young and the others from eighteen months of age. It was found that each group hunted equally well.

Hounds of seven or eight months however have proved good trackers and my own hound, the later imported Int. Ch. "Spotter of Littlebrook", was credited with an official police find when, at nine months of age, he was taken off his show bench to hunt and find a lost child.

An alternative method is, if one is available, to train your hound throughout with a steady experienced hound, and work them together until the new hound grasps the work and can be gradually eased into doing it for himself.

Your final training and practice should be in a manner so that your hound works as he will have to do at a Working Trial. Should he be called upon to do a real job it may be possible to create somewhat similar starting conditions and, as your hound gets really competent, you can try letting him get his scent from unusual objects in strange conditions. On some occasions try and get him to hunt a line without first having smelt something that has been in contact with his quarry. This is important as in police work it is frequently found that there is no article from which to give the hound his scent.

WORKING TRIALS

Working Trials, at which hounds hunt singly, and each hunt is assessed against the other in order to decide the best performance, are quite frequently held under Kennel Club rules.

The art of the Bloodhound following the scent of man

is variably referred to as hunting, working, trailing or tracking; and whichever word is used it is grand to know that efforts are made to see that these hounds never become purely ornamental. Every kennel operating as such should make sure that working ability is not lost during the search for show bench winners. A real balance must be struck between looks and working ability, and any person seeking one of these qualities and disregarding the other is doing a great disservice to the breed.

Before a hound can be entered at a Working Trial it has to have a Working Certificate. These certificates, the conditions for which vary, are not hard to obtain and application for the award of one must be made to the club organising the Trial who will arrange for an official to see your hound at work, and who will decide if your hound is good enough for the issue of a Working Certificate. Personally I feel these certificates should not be required before a hound can compete at a Trial for the tests and conditions for them are often quite difficult to arrange and they are sometimes the one thing that prevent people making entries.

Those in favour of these Working Certificates say they are needed to make certain that hounds entered at a Trial will hunt and will not riot. The argument against this is quite simple, for a hound may well behave impeccably one day and on another with a breast high scent, and the wind under his stern, may well riot for a moment. Even the best disciplined pack of Foxhounds will, on occasion, show riot.

I feel every viewpoint would be met if the need for a Working Certificate prior to Trials was done away with and all hounds were required to be hunted on a line until they had shown their steadiness in the Novice Stake.

At Trials there are usually three Stakes, the conditions for which are usually as follows:

> *Novice Stake*—lines half an hour cold, one mile long.
> *Junior Stake*—lines one hour cold, two miles long.
> *Senior Stake*—lines two hours cold, three miles long.

When judging these Stakes the quality and closeness of the work, and the time factors, are taken into consideration, and in the latter two Stakes an award is often made for the best identification. To identify his quarry the hound must go to him and place his forefeet against the chest of the hunted person. (At one time the runners who were used to train hounds carried leather bags containing meat hanging from their necks!)

A new rule has recently been introduced at Trials which says:

> Hounds may be entered in one Stake only and that one to be the lowest for which they are eligible. Nominations may be sent for entry into one other Stake. If there are vacancies, a draw will be made from among the nominations.

The reason for this is that it has been considered necessary that entries should be limited, but one cannot but feel that it is not an ideal situation. More especially it is not ideal when Kennel Club Tracking Certificates are on offer.

I well remember some years ago before these Kennel Club Tracking Certificates were reintroduced that Mr. Townson's bitch " Scarcity " refused to start hunting in the Junior Stake on the first day, but in the Senior Stake on the subsequent day hunted very well and won this Senior Stake, thus proving herself the best hound at the Trial. Under the new rule this bitch would have been ineligible for the Stake she so brilliantly won.

A further point is that when a person travels perhaps some hundreds of miles with a hound they want to get as much personal hunting as possible and it is a bit hard to have to travel a long distance for one mile's hunting in a Novice Stake with a hound capable of better things. It might also happen that for several Novice Stakes in succession an excellent hound could be unlucky enough to be drawn when scent was non-existent, while a less capable hound might get good scenting conditions.

The people who organize these Trials do however put in a vast amount of work and effort without any thought or hope of reward and our grateful thanks are due to them . . . but only by constructive criticism can we progress.

The normal procedure at Trials is for the runner to give a guide to his starting line by placing a stick vertically in the ground and another some twenty yards or so further on and at this second stick an article carrying the runner's scent is left so that the huntsman can let his hound get the scent of his quarry.

K. C. TRIAL RULES

(*By courtesy of the Kennel Club.*)

1. *Entries*—Hounds must be named at the time of making entries, and particulars given in accordance with Kennel Club Working Trial Rule 1.

2. *Order of Running*—At a date prior to the meeting, previously announced, a draw shall take place to determine the order in which hounds shall be run. By mutual agreement owners may vary the order of running, subject to the approval of the stewards.

3. *Qualifying Rounds*—In the case of a large number of entries being received, a Committee may arrange for preliminary qualifying rounds to be worked off at dates prior to the actual meeting, when hounds winning in the earlier rounds will be brought together.

4. *Disqualification for Absence*—The Committee shall announce the hour for beginning each day, and each hound must be brought up in its proper turn without delay. If absent for more than half an hour when called, a hound shall be liable to be disqualified by the judge or judges.

5. *Method of Working*—The Committee may arrange for hounds to be run singly or together in any numbers, provided the conditions are duly announced in the schedule. Hounds must be hunted by owners or their deputies. All hounds entered in any one Stake shall be tried in the same way.

6. *Hounds may be Required to Wear Collars*—Hounds when hunted together shall wear distinguishing collars if ordered by the judge or judges.

7. *Certificates*—No hound shall be entitled to win a Kennel Club Working Certificate unless he has clearly identified the runner to the satisfaction of the judge or judges.

Plate XIII

(left)

One of Mrs. G. A. Woodall's 'Ben Jairg' exports to the U.S.A.

Photo by P. A.—Reuter.

(below)

Am. Ch. "Appeline Hemlock" owned by Mr. Kent McClelland of the American Bloodhound Club.

Photo by Evening Citizen.

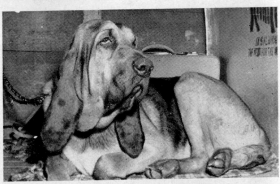

Mr. J. Gilissen's rtus Pack, which fox in Holland.

Plate XIV

Dr. Ballard's Can. Ch.
" Appeline Barsheen Huntsman "
smells his last English Spring.

Photo by Daily Sketch

Mr. G. L. Gilkey of Wisc
with
one of his working Bloodho

Mrs. N. Lindsey
and Ch.
" The Ring's Imp "
winning Hound group
under Dr. A. A. Mitten,
Duso K.C., June, 1958.

Photo by Shafer.

HUNTING AIDS

When hunting your hound ' dress the ship '—whether it be a practice hunt, Working Trial or the real thing—give the hound, and any spectators there may be, a sense of occasion. I like to see hound, huntsman and Field Trial judges properly turned out. It looks good, gives a sense of prestige to the breed, and probably even improves hound work.

For spectators at a hunt, warm light clothing such as worn by Beaglers is the most suitable, with of course the provision of a change of shoes and stockings. The huntsman, from practical experience, will have found the best attire but it is attractive and practical if he has decided to wear the uniform I describe. This enables spectators and anyone assisting in judging the hunt to see him clearly, gives him more status when a guest on someone's land, and can convey to the hound that a job of real work is afoot.

If the huntsman is fit and handles his hound closely, or hunts him on a line, then the tennis shoes as favoured by the majority of Beaglers are a must. For the others stout boots are best. Woollen stockings to suit the hunt coat and white breeches always look smart and a hunt coat modified to suit the job completes the picture. These items need not cause financial dismay as hunting clothes can be obtained secondhand for a modest cost. If you can't or don't want to dress up do not let this deter you from hunting your hounds but I put it forward as a suggestion because it has those advantages already stated . . . and anyway it adds a bit of colour to life.

H

The Horn

In the advice on training hounds it is recommended to use the voice and the horn. When using the voice to direct, cheer or rate your hound, use it loud and clear, exude confidence even if you don't feel it in your heart: go and listen to a good professional, hunting Foxhounds and get some hints; practice at home on your horn and work out some calls to suit your hound and yourself. It would be nice if the breed clubs could jointly draw up some hound music to be used as standard when hunting Bloodhounds.

The best hunting horn to use is the straight horn, which came into being at the end of the seventeenth century. Fashioned of copper with a German silver mouthpiece, it is some eight to twelve inches long. One note only can be obtained, usually ' D ' but sometimes ' A ', but whatever note is given, it makes no difference to the calls.

The purpose of the horn is twofold—it informs the Field of what is going on, and directs the hounds. Music from a hunting horn, well blown, is a wonderful thing but to be a virtuoso on such a horn is an ability given to but a few. Most huntsmen are forced to make the best use of their limited abilities.

The calls are made by varying the length of note and of the pauses between the notes. The traditional measures and their modern variations are often adapted by each huntsman to suit his own abilities. For those who cannot use the ordinary horn, there is the reed horn which is easier to blow and contains a metal reed. The note from these horns is possibly a little tinnier and does not carry quite so far as that of the straight through

variety, but they are a boon to some and prove satis-
factory.

THE HARNESS

For early training an adjustable butterfly type of harness made of soft webbing is adequate. A handyman or
needle-woman can soon make one of these. Take a 3-
inch length of webbing and sew a strong ring at the
centre of it to attach the hook of the hunting line. Place
a length of webbing against the breast-bone, take it back
across the shoulders, under and around the chest, and
when it meets cross over and return to the breast-bone.
The point where the cross over is made should be marked
and the small piece of webbing containing the ring should
be sewn on so that the loose end can eventually pass
through a gap in the stitching. A buckle should be sewn
on one end of the webbing and sufficient length left spare
on the other end to allow for growth in the hound.

The final harness should be made of soft strong
leather by a saddler and as they are quite expensive,
should not be purchased until the hound is a year old.
Even then ample provision for adjustments should be
allowed. The best type of harness should not be too
heavy and is constructed as follows. Made of leather
straps, 1—1½ inches wide, it should consist of two long
lengths; one to be placed around the chest, fastening with
an adjustable buckle, while the second strap must reach
from the top of the chest strap, around the breast-bone
and return to the original point, both ends joining the
chest strap with adjustable buckles. Between these two
buckles the rung, to which the line is to be fixed, should
be attached. Another length of leather should be attached to the strap at the point of the breast-bone, taken

back and joined to the chest strap with a loop so that it can be slipped from side to side according to the length required in the chest strap; it is advisable to have this centre strap in two pieces, fastening with another adjustable buckle, so that it can be let out if the hound increases in length.

A few ornamental studs enhance the appearance of a harness and the leather should be frequently treated to keep it soft and supple.

The various advantages and disadvantages of hunting a hound on a line or cord will soon become apparent. There are occasions when a line is essential as it is of little use if the hound finds his quarry while the huntsman has lost touch and does not know where he is. The main purpose of the line when used with a trained hound is to slow down the pace and keep huntsman and hound together. For example, it would be of little use to hunt a hound without a line if there was a heavy mist or fog.

The line to be used when the hound is to be hunted this way can be of leather, suitable line (good quality clothes line is excellent) or webbing with a strong rust-proof quick-release hook mounted on an efficient swivel. The most suitable length of line is a matter of great controversy and must depend on the individual hound. A hound hunting really steadily and close can be worked on quite a short line, but these considerations are further discussed elsewhere.

The whip, a hunting crop with a shortish thong and efficient lash, can be a great aid. I recommend all those hunting Bloodhounds to carry one. The noise from the crack of a thong and lash carries a long way and the sound can be used to emphasise instructions to your hound should he be tardy in obeying the voice or the horn, while it is also a help in turning cattle or cur dogs should they be likely to interfere with the hunt. The crook of the crop is of great assistance when hurriedly crossing ditches or climbing banks and going through wire. It also completes the picture of an equipped and competent huntsman.

THE HUNTSMAN

The foregoing are the aids to the huntsman; but the huntsman must be the aid—though never the essential aid—to the hound.

In every form of hunting the greats among huntsmen are born not made, but as with Foxhounds, Harriers or Beagles, care, thought and application to the job can, to a large degree, compensate for flair. At home or in the kennel a firm understanding and confidence must be built up between hound and huntsman; in the Field the huntsman should put 100 per cent trust in the hound's nose and only endeavour to assist the hound when he is really at a loss.

To illustrate this point let me refer to a Working Trial of some three or four years ago. This Trial took place in some extensive woodland divided by rides. A novice huntsman had his hound who was going exceptionally well on a line and the hound was steadily and confidently taking the line up the second of a number of rides turning right handed. After the hound had hunted some way up the ride a judge, after consulting the map of the lines, rode up to the huntsman and said the hound was at fault. Instead of raising his cap and saying ' I trust the hound, ma'am ' the handler lifted the reluctant hound and went to a point indicated by the judge. From then on the hound could not own the line at all and it was later found that the judge had mis-read the map. I relate this not as a criticism of any judge but to stress the need to trust the hound's nose.

It is a bad mistake to lift a hound too quickly or too often for such action will make a hound uncertain and it will look to the huntsman rather than persevere. Only lift the hound when the line is *really* lost and then only when there is a very good chance of your putting it right.

Always put yourself in the position of the quarry or runner and cast your hound to a line you think may be the most likely one. The simplest example of this is when a hound hunts through a gate into an enclosure and throws up: if the enclosure has another gate, and is surrounded by an impenetrable hedge or fence, the obvious thing to do is to cast the hound first at the other exit. Never let your own attention wander: it is always essential that you know exactly where your hound was last absolutely sure of the line, for when all else fails in your casting this is the point to which you go back. It is also always essential that you know where your hound has cast himself for if valuable time is to be saved you must first cast where the hound has not himself been. You must cast quickly and boldly with wide sweeps but ease the hound into a cast rather than really unsettle him. If you have to take the hound well back along the line to make a cast then one made in the form of a figure eight will often bring results.

The hound having lost the line and the first essential being to find the quarry, if the huntsman can, by lifting the hound and casting him well forward, get on better terms with, or a slightly hotter scent of the hunted, then this should be done.

All the actions of the huntsman should give the hound a sense of confidence in himself, remembering always that it is the hound who has the nose.

CHAPTER VIII

GLOSSARY OF BLOODHOUND TERMS

Achilles Tendon. The tendon attaching the muscle in the second thigh to the bone below the hock.

Account for. To find and identify quarry.

Affixes. Affixes are granted to breeders on payment of initial and annual maintenance fees, for their exclusive use.

A.K.C. The American Kennel Club.

Albino. An animal with a congenital deficiency of pigment in the skin, hair and eyes.

All on. Every hound in the pack present.

Amble. A slow pace.

Angulation. The angles formed by the meeting of the bones.

Anus. Posterior opening of the alimentary canal.

Appointment. Date, time and place of the meet.

Ascob. Any solid colour other than black, including black and tan in Cocker Spaniels.

At Fault. When the hound has lost the scent.

Babble. To give tongue for no reason.

Back-track. To run heel.

Ban-dog. Dog tied by day and released at night.

Barrel. Ribs and body.

Barrel Ribs. Ribs so rounded at the sides as to interfere with the action of the elbows.

Bay. Note given by a hound.

Beefy. Having coarse, heavy and bulging muscles, especially of the hindquarters.

Bitch. Female dog.

Blaze. White mark running from nose, up the head between the eyes.

Bloom. Gloss of coat.

Bone. Limbs being strong.

Brace. Two dogs of the same breed. A class for two exhibits of the same breed, owned by one person or partners. To enter this class both dogs must have been entered in some class other than the brace.

Brace Mate. A dog competing in a brace.

Brisket. Lower part of the body, between the forelegs in front of the chest.

Brood Bitch. Female dog kept for the purpose of breeding.

Brush. Tail well covered with hair, bushy like that of a fox.

Butterfly Nose. A nose with flesh-coloured sections showing through the black.

Canine. Any animal of the genus *Canis*, which includes dogs, wolves and jackals. Having the nature and qualities of a dog.

Canine Tooth. The long tooth immediately behind the incisors on each side of the jaw.

Carry the Horn. To be the huntsman.

Carry a Line. To follow scent well.

Cast. Attempt to recover scent.

Castrate. To surgically remove the testes of the male.

Castrato or a Castrate. A castrated male.

Cat Foot. Compact, well knuckled up foot, as that of a cat.

Challenge Certificate. An award given by the Kennel Club for the best exhibit of sex in a breed at a championship show, subject to the exhibit being worthy of the title of Champion.

Championship Stake. Stake where a Kennel Club Working Trial Certificate is offered.

Check. When hounds have temporarily lost the scent.

Cheeky. Rounded muscular padding at the sides of the skull.

Chest. Part of the body between the brisket and belly.

China Eye. A wall eye.

Chiselled. Muzzle well modelled to conform to the Standard of the breed.

Chops. Mouth, jaws, lips.

Cloddy. Low and thick set with large bones and heavy muscle.

Clean Boot. Natural scent of man, not strengthened by artificial aids.

Clean Hound. Without faults.

Close Coupled. The distance between withers and hip bones comparatively short.

Close Hound. One able to deal with difficult scenting conditions and keep to the line.

Coarse. Voice of poor quality or hound of too heavy a type.

Cobby. Compactly made.

Cold. Age of line, for example, ' One hour cold ' means one hour old.

Cold Line. An old scent.

Conformation. Form and structure of the hound.

Conjunctiva. Membrane lining the inner surface of the eyelid.

Couple. Two hounds.

Coupling. Leash or chain for holding two hounds.

Couplings. The body between the withers and hip bones.

Cow-hocked. Hocks turned inwards. A serious fault.

Crank Tail. A short twisted tail.

Crash. Pack giving tongue together.

Cries. Traditional hunting field words or phrases.

Crossbred. A dog whose sire and dam are of two different breeds.

Croup. The back above the hind limbs. Line from pelvis to set on of stern.

Crown. The highest part of the head.

Crupper. The croup.

Cry. Voice of hound when on a line.

Cryptorchid. A male animal in which the testicles are not visibly apparent.

Cull. To eliminate unwanted hounds.

Cur Dog. Any dog met whilst hunting, apart from hounds taking part.

Dapple. Marked with small spots on white or grey ground.

Dentition. Number, kind, form and arrangement of teeth.

Dew-claw. Extra claw on the inside, lower portion of the legs.

Dewlap. Loose pendulous skin under the throat.

Dish Face. Nose higher than the base of the stop—concave.

Disqualification. Fault for which a dog is not permitted to compete in a show, Trial or Stake.

Distemper Teeth. Discoloration and pitting resulting from a disease.

Double. When quarry runs close to, or back on, his tracks.

Double Coat. Undercoat plus outer, with the longer coat growing through.

Down in Pastern. Forelegs bent at the pastern.

Draft. Hounds passed on from one pack to another.

Drag. Scent laid by artificial means, such as a sheep's paunch.

Draw. Search for quarry's line. Call hounds from kennel singly.

Dry. Free from surplus skin or flesh about the mouth, lips or throat.

Dudley Nose. Brown or flesh-coloured nose, often accompanied by eye-rims of a similar colour.

Dwell. When hounds do not drive forward.

Elbow. Joint at the top of the foreleg, next to the body.

Enter. To initiate a young hound in the art of hunting.

Ewe Neck. Thin neck having insufficient, faulty or concave arch.

Expression. Combination of features of the head, particularly eyes, producing an impression.

Faking. To change the appearance of a dog artificially.

Fang. Canine or eye tooth.

Fault. A point of poor conformation or technique.

Fault. A hound is at fault when hunting the wrong line.

Feather. Hound waving his stern when not sure enough to speak on a faint scent.

Fetlock. Joint between pastern and lower arm.

Field. People following the hunt.

Field, In the. The place where the hound works at hunting by scent.

Field Trial. Working Trial.

Filled Right Up. An unchiselled muzzle.

Flat Sided. Having insufficient spring of rib.

Flews. Pendulous inner corners of the lips of the upper jaw.

Flyer. A notably excellent specimen.

Foil. A scent obliterating that of quarry.

Forearm. Front leg between elbow and pastern.

Fore-face. Muzzle.

Fore-hand. Front of the dog, excluding the head.

Front. Fore-hand.

Full Cry. Hounds giving tongue on a good line.

Game. Quarry.

Gay Tail. Tail carried higher than the approved carriage.

Give Tongue. Hound using his voice.

Go to Cry. Hounds going to other hounds who are giving tongue.

Good Doer. Hound who eats well, and shows well being as a result.

Grizzle. Light hairs with dark tips, usually grey.

Gaskin. Second thigh.

Hackney Action. The front feet lifted high in movement.

Handler. Huntsman. Person showing hound.

Hare Foot. Long narrow foot.

Hark Forward. Shout to indicate that hound has spoken.

Hark In. Term used to instruct hound to go to another who has found the scent.

Haunch. The hip.

Haw. The third eyelid.

Heads Up. Term describing the action of hounds lifting their heads from the scent.

Heat.   Alternative word for season in bitches.

Heat.   Contest between a brace of hounds.

Heel.   Hound hunting in the opposite direction to which quarry has run.

Height.   The perpendicular measurement taken from the top of the shoulder blade to the ground.

Herring Gutted.   Slab sided.

Hind-hand.   Behind the hips, including the croup, tail, hind legs and feet.

Hit Off.   To recover the line of scent after a check.

Hock.   Lower joint of the hind leg.

Hold Hard.   Warning to the Field not to come close to the hounds.

Hold Up.   Warning to hound to stay still.

Holloa.   The shout to indicate that one of the Field has seen the quarry.

Honourable Scars.   Scars from injuries sustained whilst hound is at work.

Hound Marked.   Black, tan and white markings characteristic of a Foxhound or Beagle.

Humerus.   Bone of the upper arm.

Huntsman.   The person hunting the hound.

Identification.   Act of hound showing recognition of his particular quarry.

Inbreeding.   The mating of dogs of the same breed to those closely related.

In-shouldered.   Forelegs too close together.

Kink Tail.   Sharply bent tail.

Knuckling Over.   Front legs bulging forward at the pastern joint.

Lay on. To start hounds on a scent.

Lift. To take hound off the line he is hunting.

Line. Scent of quarry.

Line. Cord, tape or strap attached to harness of hound when hunting.

Line. Course taken by runner at a Working Trial.

Line Breeding. The mating of dogs of the same breed within their own family, for example, the mating of a bitch to her grandsire.

Loaded. Superfluous padding.

Loins. On either side of the spinal column, between the hip bone and false ribs.

Loose. To hunt a hound loose is to hunt it free of a line.

Lower Arm. Foreleg between the elbow and pastern joint.

Lumber. Superfluous flesh or muscle.

Lumbering. An awkward gait.

Mating. Putting together the male and female for the purpose of reproduction.

Molar Tooth. A rear tooth, used for grinding.

Mongrel. A dog carrying the blood of three or more breeds.

Monorchid. A male animal having but one testicle in the scrotum.

Moving Off. When hounds are taken from the meet to the first draw.

Mute. Hound following scent without giving tongue.

Muzzle. Foremost part of the face.

Nape. Back of the neck, at the junction with the head.

Nomination. Entry made in a Stake, subject to special conditions laid down by Committee.

Nose. A hound who follows scent well is said to have a ' good nose '.

Occiput. Prominent bone at the peak of the skull.

Œstrum. The period during which a bitch may be mated.

Olfactory. Of, or pertaining to, the sense of smell.

Open. When hounds begin to give tongue.

Out at Elbows. Elbows turned outwards from the body.

Out at Shoulder. Shoulder blades loosely attached to the body.

Outcrossing. The mating of unrelated dogs.

Overshot. The front teeth of the upper jaw projecting over those of the lower jaw.

Own. When hound ' owns ' a line he has found it.

Pace. A gait in which the legs move in lateral pairs, the animal supported alternatively by the right and left legs.

Pack. A number of hounds kept together for the purpose of hunting as a team.

Pad. Foot of hound.

Paddling. Throwing the fore feet sideways when in action.

Paper Foot. Shallow foot with thin pads.

Pastern. Foreleg, between the fetlock and the foot.

Peak. Another name for the Occiput.

Pied. Term used for a coat of two colours in irregular patches and of unequal proportions.

Pig Jawed. Overshot.

Pipe-stopper Tail. Tail with inadequate substance.

Point of Shoulder. Junction of upper arm with shoulder blades.

Pottering Hound.   One making no progress on scent.
Prefix.   An affix added *before* a hound's name.
Puppy.   A dog under twelve months of age.

Quality.   Refinement.
Quarters.   The two hind legs.

Racy.   Long in legs and body, slightly built.
Rangy.   Tall and elongated, but with greater substance than ' racy '.
Rate.   Scold.
Rat Tail.   Tail with short smooth hair.
Reachy.   Covering much ground between the fore and hind feet.
Ring Tail.   Tail carried in a circle over the back.
Ringer.   A dog closely resembling another dog.
Riot.   To hunt anything other than the original quarry.
Roach Back.   An arched back.
Roman Nose.   The bridge of the nose so high as to form a convex line from forehead to tip of nose.
Runner.   Person laying line for a hunt.

Saddle Back.   Sway back.
Scale of Points.   A table attached to a breed Standard, setting forth the relative percentage value for perfection in the various parts of the body.
Scapula.   Shoulder blade.
Scent.   Smell given off by quarry.
Scissors Bite.   The incisors of the upper jaw just overlap those of the lower jaw.
Season.   A term for the period of œstrum.
Second Thigh.   The gaskin.
Self Colour.   A single colour.

Plate XV

(left)

Ch. " Easebourne Argos " owned by Detec.-Sgt. Erik E. Pettersson of Oedeshoeg, Sweden—Mr. Pettersson has the largest kennel and trains hounds for the Swedish police.

(below)

Mr. Poul Lassen with Ch. " Buxhall Annette ", Mr. Pettersson with " Astor's Donna Urvana ", and Mr. Herluf Anderson with " Hazel of Brighton ", at the Danish K.C. show, Copenhagen, November, 1958.

Photo by Vittus Nielsen.

Plate XVI

Photo by] [*Boland.*

Puppies out of Ch. " Bonnie ",
owned by Mr. and Mrs. Boland of New York.

Courtesy of] (*Rank Organisation.*

British television comedian Benny Hill and Ch. " Hector " on the trail—
with apologies to Sexton Blake and " Pedro "—in the Michael Balcon-
Ealing Studios production ' Who Done It ? '

Septum.   Muscular wall dividing the nostrils.

Settle.   To get hound hunting steadily.

Shelly.   Narrow body, lacking bone and substance.

Shots.   Injections.

Sickle Hocks.   Hocks so bent that the part below them is placed forward and not vertical.

Skirter.   Hound who takes short cuts rather than follow the correct line of the quarry.

Slab sides.   Insufficient spring of rib.

Snipy.   Muzzle pointed and weak.

Spay.   Surgical removal of the ovaries, rendering a bitch sterile.

Splay Foot.   Flat foot with spreading toes.

Split.   Hounds, when hunting other than singly, separate and follow different scents.

Squirrel Tail.   Tail curving forward over the back.

Stake.   Competitive hunting at a Field Trial.

Stale Line.   When quarry has passed a long while beforehand.

Stance.   Manner of standing.

Staring Coat.   Hair dry and harsh, standing off from the body.

Stern.   Tail.

Stifle.   In the hind leg, above the hock.

Stilted.   Uneven gait.

Stop.   The depression between the eyes, at the junction of the nose and skull.

Straight Hocks.   Hocks not bent.

Straight Shoulders.   Shoulder blades too upright.

Strain.   Bloodlines or Pedigree.

Stud Book.   A registry in which a record of age, pedigree, name of breeder and owner of each hound is kept.

Style.   Quality of working.

I

Substance. Strength of skeleton.
Suffix. An affix added *after* a hound's name.
Sway Back. Sagging spine.
Swing. Cast about in an attempt to recover a line.

Tail Hounds. Hounds at the rear of a pack.
Teapot Tail. Tail curved resembling a teapot handle.
Texture. Nature of coat.
Throaty. Superfluous skin under the throat.
Throw their Tongues. When hounds speak or give
    tongue.
Throws Up. When a hound loses the line.
Tight Mouthed. Lacking sufficient voice.
Timber. A dog excelling in bone, especially of the legs,
    is said to have good timber.
Tongue. To give voice when on the scent.
Tricolour. A coat of three colours, usually black-white-
    and-tan.
Tuck-up. The waist.
Type. The characteristic qualities of a breed.

Undercoat. Short fine hairs concealed by a longer
    top growth.
Underhung. Undershot.
Undershot. Having the lower front teeth projecting be-
    yond the uppers.
Upper Arm. Between the elbow and shoulder.

Varmint. Wicked expression.
Vent. The anus.

Walking. The process of putting out puppies bred
    in a kennel, to be reared with absolute freedom.
Wall Eye. A blue eye.

'Ware Riot.   Shout to stop hounds hunting anything
other than the original quarry.

Weaving.   Front legs crossing when in action.

Weediness.   Lack of bone and substance.

Well Sprung.   Rounded and well-formed ribs.

Whelping.   The act of a bitch giving birth.

Whelps.   Puppies.

Whipper-in.   Servant who assists the huntsman.

Withers.   Between the shoulder blades at the base of the
neck.

Working a Line.   Following a scent.

Working Certificate.   One required before a hound can
compete at a Field Trial.

Wrinkle.   Loose skin on the forehead and sides of the
face.

CHAPTER IX

HOUND NAMES

It has always been traditional with Bloodhounds, as with most other hounds that hunt by scent, for the old established hound names to be used. These are often affixed by the breeder's or owner's kennel name being added before or after the hound's own name.

Examples of the prefix are " *Buxhall* Henrietta " or " *Rytow* Helena " and of the suffix " Rosette *of Brighton* " or " Belinda *of Woodcourt* ". A number of hounds carry two prefixes, or a prefix and a suffix such as Ch. " *Appeline* Hector *of Westsummerland* " or " *Westsummerland* Crown *of Brighton* ". This occurs when a hound is bred or registered by one kennel and then goes to another kennel who pay a ' Change of Name ' Fee of £2 to the Kennel Club.

These affixes are, subject to the discretion of the Kennel Club, the sole property of the kennel owner who pays an annual maintenance or title fee for their protection. I have already given a list of Bloodhound affixes early in this book (see pages 27—28).

A selection of traditional hound names now follows. The letters I, K, Q, U, X, Y, Z, are not included as there are not very many correct hound names commencing with these letters. However, what names exist with these initial letters are included with a further selection of other names in my *Beagle Handbook* published in this series, and an additional selection is also included in my companion volume *The Basset Hound Handbook*.

All traditional hound names are ones that come easily and musically off the tongue in two syllables. It will be seen that some names are actually spelt with three syllables but they should still be pronounced with two. For example Dynamite becomes Dyn-mite, Timorous—Tim-rous, Wonderful—Wund-ful, and so on.

Please use these traditional names when christening your hounds . . . they sound *so* much more dignified than something like " Mama's Sweet Baby " or " Sweet Tiggy Toozles of Acacia Walk "!

A

Dogs	*Bitches*	*Dogs*	*Bitches*
Abbot	Abbess	Alien	Amber
Acklam	Acid	Ambush	Amorous
Ackland	Acme	Amulet	Anxious
Actor	Acorn	Antrim	April
Adrian	Adella	Arab	Arctic
Agile	Agnes	Archer	Arnica
Aimless	Agony	Arson	Artless
Alaric	Airlie	Atheist	Attila
Albany	Alice	Atlas	Auburn
Alibi	Allspice	Author	Ayah

B

Dogs	*Bitches*	*Dogs*	*Bitches*
Baccarat	Ballad	Battleaxe	Bathsheba
Badger	Balsam	Bedouin	Beeswing
Bailiff	Bandbox	Berkely	Bertha
Bajazet	Bangle	Bilberry	Billow
Baltic	Banjo	Bishop	Bittern
Bandit	Banner	Bismarck	Blackberry
Banker	Barefoot	Blacksmith	Bolero
Bardolph	Bargain	Bluebeard	Bridget
Barnaby	Baroness	Briton	Butterfly
Basilisk	Bashful	Bulrush	Buxom

C

Dogs	Bitches	Dogs	Bitches
Caesar	Cactus	Chimer	Chocolate
Caliban	Cambric	Clansman	Citron
Cannon	Candid	Clerical	Classic
Caradoc	Caramel	Clifton	Cleo
Carver	Casket	Conway	Cora
Caspian	Ceres	Cormorant	Courteous
Chairman	Charlotte	Cossack	Crocus
Charter	Chastity	Cryer	Crumpet
Chaser	Chatterbox	Culprit	Cygnet
Cheddar	Chickory	Curate	Cymbal

D

Dogs	Bitches	Dogs	Bitches
Dado	Dahlia	Draco	Donna
Daimler	Dagmar	Dragon	Dowry
Damon	Damask	Dramatist	Draggle
Darnley	Danceaway	Dreadnought	Drapery
Dastard	Dawdle	Drummer	Dreamer
Dealer	Dayfly	Dryad	Dresden
Debtor	Delia	Duelist	Drowsy
Delaware	Dizzy	Dunster	Duchess
Dodger	Doleful	Duster	Dulcet
Dolphin	Dollar	Dynasty	Dwindle

E

Dogs	Bitches	Dogs	Bitches
Earthquake	Easter	Emphasis	Ermine
Easeful	Ecstasy	Enterprise	Errant
Edify	Edict	Epilogue	Esther
Ednam	Effable	Equerry	Etiquette
Edward	Egret	Erin	Esa
Egbert	Eileen	Ethelred	Eventide
Egerton	Ellen	Eustace	Extra
Element	Elegance	Exile	Extract
Embassy	Elsie	Expert	Eyebrow
Emerson	Emily	Eyelet	Eyelash

F

Dogs	Bitches	Dogs	Bitches
Faber	Fable	Figaro	Fizzle
Fabian	Fabric	Flunkey	Flameless
Facer	Fairstar	Foiler	Flattery
Fairfax	Fallacy	Foljamb	Flicker
Falcon	Fancy	Fowler	Floral
Falmouth	Feather	Framer	Fondle
Fearless	Fernery	Franchise	Fortunate
Felix	Festival	Fraser	Foundling
Ferryman	Fiction	Friar	Freakish
Fiddler	Fiery	Fury	Furtive

G

Dogs	Bitches	Dogs	Bitches
Gabbler	Gadabout	Giant	Gratis
Gaelic	Gannet	Gideon	Grecian
Gainer	Garish	Glaucus	Gretna
Gainsborough	Gesture	Glider	Grotto
Galahad	Ghostly	Golfer	Guidance
Gamecock	Giantress	Gorgon	Guileless
Ganymede	Glamour	Grabber	Gurgle
Gaoler	Glimmer	Gudgeon	Gushing
General	Goddess	Gunner	Gwendoline
Genius	Goosestep	Guzman	Gymnast

H

Dogs	Bitches	Dogs	Bitches
Hadrian	Halma	Holloway	Honesty
Halcyon	Happiness	Hornet	Housemaid
Hamlet	Harebell	Hornpipe	Hoyden
Handel	Haughty	Hospadar	Huddle
Hangman	Hazel	Hostile	Humorous
Harborough	Heartless	Hubert	Huntress
Hebrew	Heather	Huckster	Hurtful
Hercules	Helena	Hunter	Hyacinth
Hesperus	Hindrance	Hustler	Hymnal
Highflyer	Homely	Hyssop	Hyphen

J

Dogs	Bitches	Dogs	Bitches
Jackdaw	Jaculate	Jeweller	Joyless
Jagwort	Jasmine	Jonathan	Judy
Janitor	Jaunty	Journal	Julia
Jarvey	Jenny	Journalist	Juliet
Jason	Jetty	Judgement	Jaeger
Jawbone	Jezebel	Julian	Jaguar
Jesuit	Joyful	Jupiter	Juniper

L

Dogs	Bitches	Dogs	Bitches
Laceman	Lappet	Locksmith	Locket
Lamphrey	Legacy	Locust	Logic
Lancelot	Legend	Lofty	Lonely
Landmark	Lemon	Loiterer	Lollypop
Landseer	Libertine	Logwood	Lotus
Lexicon	Lightly	Longbow	Loyalty
Liberal	Linda	Lottery	Luckless
Lincoln	Linnet	Lowlander	Lullaby
Livid	Lioness	Lucifer	Lustre
Loafer	Lissom	Luther	Lydia

M

Dogs	Bitches	Dogs	Bitches
Madman	Macaroon	Milford	Minion
Magnate	Magical	Miner	Minuet
Mallard	Malaga	Minstrel	Mistletoe
Malmesbury	Mantle	Miser	Model
Manxman	Marchioness	Mohawk	Modesty
Mariner	Margot	Monarch	Moleskin
Marksman	Mayfly	Moralist	Moonbeam
Meddler	Medley	Mullet	Mournful
Memnon	Melba	Munster	Muslin
Merchant	Merciful	Musket	Mystery

N

Dogs	Bitches	Dogs	Bitches
Native	Namesake	Nobbler	Nightingale
Nautilus	Naphtha	Norseman	Nina
Neptune	Neatly	Normal	Noiseless
Nero	Nebula	Norwood	Nonsense
Neutral	Nidda	Notable	Noonday
Nickleby	Needless	Notary	Novelty
Niggard	Negress	Novelist	Novice
Nightwatch	Nettle	Nugget	Nursling
Nihilist	Nicety	Number	Nutriment
Nipperkin	Nightgown	Nuneham	Nutshell

O

Dogs	Bitches	Dogs	Bitches
Oakley	Oakleaf	Onslow	Orange
Oasis	Occult	Oppidam	Orbit
Odeon	Ocelot	Orient	Orderly
Ogre	Offspring	Orion	Ormonde
Oiler	Ogle	Orton	Ornament
Oliver	Ongar	Oscar	Ossett
Olden	Oola	Otter	Outlook
Oldham	Option	Oulton	Overture
Olney	Optional	Oundle	Oxygen
Oncer	Oral	Owen	

P

Dogs	Bitches	Dogs	Bitches
Packman	Parasol	Phoenix	Petticoat
Padlock	Parchment	Pickwick	Phoebe
Paladin	Partial	Pieman	Picture
Peacock	Passionate	Pilgrim	Piety
Pegasus	Peaceful	Pirate	Placid
Pennon	Peeress	Pistol	Pleasant
Pensioner	Penitence	Plaintiff	Poetess
Peppery	Peony	Plutus	Poplin
Pessimist	Peppermint	Pompey	Porcelain
Phantom	Perdita	Prior	Prettylass

R

Dogs	Bitches	Dogs	Bitches
Raceaway	Rachel	Reprobate	Rhoda
Radium	Rapture	Resonant	Rhythm
Raeburn	Readily	Reveller	Righteous
Raftsman	Reckless	Rhetoric	Rigmarole
Raider	Redrose	Rhinewine	Rita
Rampart	Refuge	Ribald	Roguery
Ramsay	Relic	Rifleman	Rollick
Rapier	Restful	Roebuck	Roma
Remus	Reticent	Royalist	Roseleaf
Renegade	Revelry	Ruthless	Ruin

S

Dogs	Bitches	Dogs	Bitches
Sabre	Sabine	Seaman	Shelach
Sackcloth	Sacrifice	Sheriff	Sherry
Sago	Scamper	Shylock	Skylark
Salisbury	Scornful	Sinner	Slumber
Sandiway	Scruple	Solomon	Soda
Saraband	Sealskin	Spartan	Sonnet
Sattelite	Seamstress	Stalwart	Sorceress
Saxon	Shamless	Stilton	Spangle
Sceptre	Shamrock	Stoic	Spindle
Schooner	Sheba	Sultan	Symphony

T

Dogs	Bitches	Dogs	Bitches
Tablet	Taffeta	Tennyson	Treacle
Taciturn	Tanzy	Terrapin	Trespass
Tagus	Tauntress	Terrible	Trinket
Talbot	Tigress	Thunder	Troublesome
Tamper	Tiptoe	Timon	Truelass
Tangler	Toffee	Titus	Tulip
Tankard	Tomboy	Tomahawk	Tuneful
Tantalus	Topaz	Tomtom	Turquoise
Tartar	Tragic	Trapper	Twinkle
Tempter	Tranquil	Tuscan	Typical

V

Dogs	Bitches	Dogs	Bitches
Vacant	Valda	Venerable	Venus
Valet	Valid	Venom	Verity
Valorous	Valve	Venturer	Vesta
Vanadis	Vanda	Verger	Vineyard
Vanguard	Vanity	Veteran	Viola
Vantage	Variance	Viceroy	Vivian
Vapid	Varna	Victor	Vocal
Varlet	Vaultress	Violent	Voluntary
Vatican	Vehement	Vulcan	Votary
Vaulter	Vellum	Vulture	Vulpine

W

Dogs	Bitches	Dogs	Bitches
Waister	Wakeful	Weasel	Wheedle
Wakefield	Wallflower	Weathercock	Whimsey
Wallace	Wanton	Webster	Whirlpool
Warsford	Warble	Wellington	Whitethroat
Warcry	Wary	Whirlwind	Wintry
Warlike	Waspish	Whisker	Wisdom
Warpaint	Waxwork	Whistler	Wonder
Washington	Wedgwood	Witness	Woodlark
Watchful	Welcome	Wrestler	Worthless
Waterloo	Whatnot	Wyvern	Wrongful

INDEX

Afghan Hound, 1
American Bloodhound, Pl. viii
—— —— Club, 26, Pl. xiii
—— Coonhounds, Pl. vi
—— Kennel Club, 26
Anderson, Trooper, 19
——, Herluf, Pl. xv
——, Sir John and Lady (see
  Waverley, Viscount and Vis.
  countess)
  " Appeline Barsheen Hunts-
  man ", Can Ch., Pl. xiv
'—— Hector of Westsummer-
  land ", 16, 22, 43, Pls. xi, xvi
"—— Hemlock ", Am. Ch., 82,
  Pl. xiii
Appleton, Douglas, 26, Pl. x
Arnolda, B.F.N., 19
Association of Bloodhound
  Breeders, 10, 13, 25
" Astor's Donna Urvana ", Pl.
  xv

Bagot, Lord, 10
Balihead, Thomas, 5
Ballard, Dr., Pl. xiv
" Barbarossa ", Ch., Pl. iv
" Barnaby ", Ch., Pl. v
Barnsley, Evelyn, Pl. ix
" Barset of Barchester ", Ch.,
  Pl. ix
"Barsheen Bynda of Huguenot",
  14, 17, 18
" —— Jewel ", Ch., Pl. ix
Basset Hound Handbook, The,
  118
Beagle Handbook, The, 72, 88,
  118
Bean, Sawney, 4
Bell, Jacob, Pl. ii
Besson, Mme. Anne, 20
Beynon, John, 14
Blake, Sexton, Pl. xvi
" Blazer ", Ch., Pl. iv

Bloat (see Distention)
Bloodhound Breeders' Bulletin,
  19
Bloodhound Club, 10, 25, 26
—— -Otterhound crossbred, Pl.
  viii
Bloodhounds and How to Train
  Them, 46
Boellaars, L., Pl. v
Boland, Mr. and Mrs., 14, 19
" Bonnie ", Ch., Pl. xvi
Borzois, 77
Boucher, J. H., 61
Brache, 2
Breeding, 56-72
—— contracts, 57-59
Brews, Alan, 25
British Museum of Natural
  History, Pl. vi
B.S.A.V.A., 78
Brough, E., 10, 11, Pls. iv, v
Brown, Trooper, 19
Buchanan-Jardine, Sir J., 20
" Buccaneer of Brighton ", Ch.,
  77
Bulldog, The, 11
" Burgho ", Ch., Pl. v
" Burgundy ", Pl. iv
" Buxhall Annette ", Ch., Pl. xv

Canis f. leineri, 1
Cannibals, 4
Cardigan, Earl of, 26
Chapman, Capt. and Mrs.
  C. H., Pl. v
" Chatley Blazer ", Ch., Pl. vii
" —— Brilliant ", Pl. vi
" —— Regent ", 10
Chelmsford, Viscount, 26
Complete Dog Breeders,
  Manual, The, 86
" Coral of Westsummerland "
  Ch., Pl. vii
Cornell Veterinarian, 61

" Countess ", Pl. ii
Cousens (see Field and
   Cousens)
Cowen, Major, 9
Cox, Harding, 11
" Cromwell ", Ch., Pls. iv, x
Cross, Mrs. C. Ashton, 11

" Dark of Brighton ", Ch., Pl. vi
" Dasher of Brighton ", 43, Pl.
   xii
" Dauntless ", 9
" Dazzle of Reynalton ", Ch., 77
de Guise, Cardinal, 3
Deerhounds, 78
" Dingle ", 9
Distention, 77, 78-81
Dodge, Mrs. G. R., 19
Dogs of the British Islands,
   The, 9
" Dominator of Brighton ", Ch.,
   Pl. x
" Don ", Ch., 43
" Draco ", 9
" Druid ", 9, 10, Frontispiece
Dryden, J. K., 14
Dumfriesshire pack, Pl. viii
Dunn, W. H., 10
' Dusk of Westsummerland ",
   Pl. vii

Earl, Maud, Pl. x
" Easebourne Argos ", Ch.,
   Pl. xv
" ——— Tarquin ", D. Ch., Pl.
   xii
East, Henry, 11, 26
Edmunds, Mrs. C. C., 11
Edwards, Sydenham, Pl. i
Egyptian Greyhound, 1
Elizabeth I, 3
—— II, 24
Elms, Mrs. N. E., 11, 25
" Emily of Westsummerland ",
   Ch., Pl. vii
Emms, Pl. vii
Eugene, Prince, Frontispiece
Eyelids, Inverted, 81-83

Farman, Edgar, 11
Faversham, Lord, 9
Feeding, 72-76
Field, The, 6
Field and Cousens, Messrs., 10
Finkle, Mrs., 6, 7
——, Tom, 6, 7
Foote, R. H., 61
Foxhounds, 17, 42
Furness, Mr. and Mrs. R., Pl.
   ix

Gélibert, J. B., Frontispiece
Gilkey, Geo. L., Pl. xiv
Gillissen, J., 20, Pl. xiii
Glossary of Terms, 105-117
Goddard, G. B., Pl. 1
Golden Retriever, 1
" Grafton ", Pl. ii
Great Dane, 78
Greyhounds of St. Louis, 3
Greyhounds, 23
Grooming, 85-88

Harness, The, 101-102
Harrison, F. C., 45
Haw, 82
" Hazel of Brighton ", Pl. xv
Henderson, D., 20, Pl. xi
Henry IV, 3
Heydon, Miss S. T., 10
Hill, Benny, 22, Pl. xvi
Holford, C. E., 9, 11
Horn, The, 100-101
Houghton, ' Cy ', 19
Hounds of the World, 20
House training, 48-50
Hubbard, Clifford, v, 86
Hubert, Francois, 2
Humphries, Mrs. S. A., 10
Hunting aids, 99-104
Hutton, Sir William, 5
Hylden, Mr. and Miss, 11, 77,
   Pls. vi, x

Importations, Post-war, 13-20
Infra-red lamp, 65
Irish Wolfhounds, 77, 78

James I, 3, 4
Jenkins, Dr., 19
Jennings, T. A., 9, 10
Judges, 44

Kennel Club, v, 10, 11, 24-25, 58, 59, 96, 97, 118
Kennel Club Stud Book, 10
—— *Encyclopædia, The*, 11
Kirk, R. W., 61
Krehl, G. R., Pl. iv

Landseer, Sir Edwin, Pl. ii
Langdale, Mrs. A. M., 25, Pl. xii
Lassen, Poul, 19, Pl. xv
" Laura ", Pl. ii
Lead training, 51-53
Lee, Belinda, 22
——, Rawdon Briggs, 45
Leeds, Duke of, 8
Legard, Sir Charles, 10
" Leo of Reynalton ", 11
Limier, 2
Lindsey, Mrs. N., Pl. xiv
Lloyd, H. S., Pl. viii
" Luath XI ", Pl. iv

McClelland, A. Kent, 26, Pl. xiii
Mangin, Mrs. S. H., 11
Manhunts, 3-8, 18, 19
" Margrave ", Ch., Pl. v
Martinez, 20
Mating, 60-62
Measurements, 42-43
" Melody of Westsummerland ", 16
Melville, Whyte, 12, 46
Mitten, Dr. A. A., Pl. xiv
Mitra, Mrs. S. K., 19
Moneypenny, C. J. B., 11
Moore, R. H., Pl. v
Movement, 37-38
Mullikin, V. G., 18
Mummery, D., 20

Names, Selected, 119-125
——, Teaching, 50, 51
Napoleon, Prince, 9, *Frontispiece*
Nichol, C. S., 43, Pl. xii
" Nick Carter ", 18, Pl. vii
Noerr, Mr. and Mrs. Lees, 19
Norman, Mr. and Mrs., 15

Oldfield, Mrs. Rosamund, 14, 43, Pl. xii
Oldman, Mrs. Yvonne, v, 77, Pl. ix
Oliphant, Mr. and Mrs. 10, 11, 26, 45, Pl. vii
Origin and Early History, 1-12

" Panther ", Pl. iv
Papillon Handbook, The, 66
Pease, J. W., 9
" Pedro ", Sexton Blake's, Pl. xvi
Pekingese, 11
Pekingese Dog, The, 11
—— *Handbook, The*, 11
Pettersson, Erik, 19, Pl. xv
Pisanello, 2
" Pluto of Dobrudden ", Aust. Ch., Pl. xi
Points, Breed, 38-42
—— to look for, 70-71
Prefixes, Leading, 27-28
Puppy, Care of, 67-69

" Rapid ", 10
Ray, Reynold, 9
" Baycroft Jailer ", W.T. Ch., Pl. ix
Records, Bloodhound, 23-24
" Regent ", 9
Reinagle, Pl. i
Rivière, Briton, Pl. iii
Roberts, Peggy and Bob Russell, 66
" Roswell ", 9
Rothschild, Baron, 9
Routledge, Thomas, 5, 6
Russian Tracker, 1
Ryan, Mrs. 19

Sadleir, Mrs. M., 11, Pl. ix
St. Hubert Hound, 1, 2-3
——John, Mrs. Harris, 11, 14
Sandeman, H. G. H., Pl. iv
" Scarcity of Kelperland ", 96,
    Pl. xi
Scarlett, Jake, 10
Sleuth Hound, 1, 2
' Slouth dogs ', 5, 6
Smith, A. Croxton, 11, 45, Pl.
    iv
Somerville, 11
" Spotter of Littlebrook ", Int.
    Ch., 14-15, 77, Pl. xii
Standard, 29-32
——, American, 32-35
——, Analysis of, 35-37
Stocker, H., 26
' Stonehenge ' (see Walsh, J. H.)
Stratton, Rev. G., Pl. iv

Talbot Hound, 1, 2, 12
Taunton, W. K., 11
Temperament, 83-85
" The Ring's Imp ", Am. Ch.,
    Pl. xiv
Thomas, Will, 19

Tinker, J. C., 10
Tomarctos, 1
Townson, R. S., 26, 78, 96, Pl.
    xi
Training, 48-55, 89
—— to hunt, 89-94
Trials, 94-97
——, Rules for, 97-98
Turner, J. Sidney, 11

" Voltigeur ", 6, 7, 8

Walsh, J. H., 9
Waverley, Viscount and Vis-
    countess, 11, 14, 16, 17, Pl.
    vii
" Welcome ", 9
"Westsummerland Montgomery
    of Bre-Mar-Har-Ros ", 14,
    16-17
Whelping, 65-67
Whitney, Leon, 19, 46, 78, 82
Wilson, Leo, 14
Woodall, Mrs. G. A., Pl. xiii
" Wuthering Dulciana of Dob-
    rudden ", Aust. Ch., Pl. xi